9 X 8/08 (2/02) LC

American Ways

D0029132

LV

★ ★ ★

American Ways

A Guide for Foreigners in the United States

Gary Althen

Intercultural Press, Inc.

Yarmouth, Maine

Library of Congress Cataloging-in-Publication Data

Althen, Gary.
  American ways.

  Bibliography: p.
  1. United States—Description and travel—
1981-   —Guide-books. 2. Visitors, Foreign—
United States—Guide-books. 3. Aliens—United
States—Guide-books. 4. Intercultural communi-
cation. I. Title.
E158.A46 1988   917.3'04927   87-46023
ISBN 0-933662-68-8

For information, address Intercultural Press, Inc.,
PO Box 768, Yarmouth, Maine 04096.

Printed in the United States of America

Contents

Preface

This book was drafted while I was living temporarily in Malaysia. I was on a year's leave of absence from my position as a foreign student adviser at the University of Iowa. Being outside my own country gave me some of the opportunities I tell foreign students they have when they come to Iowa. It gave me a different perspective on my own country, a clearer view of how life there compares with life elsewhere. It gave me the opportunity to see other Americans act as foreigners. It helped me, in short, to crystallize many ideas about the distinguishing aspects of American culture.

The ideas and examples in this book come mainly from the hundreds of conversations I have had with foreign students and scholars I have met in the United States. In addition, they come from reading, from my own experiences as a foreigner, from hearing stories other Americans have told, and from watching Americans' reactions to foreigners. I have seen patterns in people's responses—ideas and behavior that recur. In this book I have tried to organize, summarize, and discuss those patterns in a way that I believe will be helpful to visitors from other countries.

Other observers might have noticed different things or interpreted them in different ways. Other writers might include things I have left out or leave out things I have put in. They might emphasize different points. Readers should recognize that this book presents one person's views. The ideas in here are starting points for observation, thought, and discussion. They are not conclusions.

I undertook this book with the encouragement of David

Hoopes and Peggy Pusch of the Intercultural Press. Their support I gratefully acknowledge. Three colleagues at the University of Iowa were good enough to read the entire manuscript and offer suggestions for its improvement. They are Stephen Duck (who is from England), Christiane Hartnack (from Germany), and Virginia Gross. Two other colleagues, Theresa GanglGhassemlouei and Kay Turney, helped with particular chapters. Dave Hoopes, Kay Hoopes, and Judy Carl Hendrick— all with Intercultural Press—made detailed editorial and substantive suggestions. My wife, Sandy, lent moral support through the writing and revisions. All these people helped make this a better book than it would have been had I undertaken it alone.

Most of the credit for this book goes to the countless people who have talked to me about their reactions to Americans. I cannot even begin to name them, but I appreciate them all.

Gary Althen

Introduction

Most Americans see themselves as open, frank, and fairly friendly. If you ask them a question, they will answer it. They have nothing to hide. They cannot understand why people from other countries should have any difficulty understanding them. Unless, of course, there are language problems.

But most foreigners do have trouble understanding Americans. Even if they have a good command of English, most foreigners have at least some difficulty understanding what the Americans they encounter are thinking and feeling. What ideas and attitudes underlie their actions? What motivates them? What makes them talk and act the way they do? This book addresses those questions. The book is intended to help foreign visitors—both those staying for a long time and those here for short visits—understand the natives.

ON "UNDERSTANDING"

This book is not intended to encourage foreigners to like Americans or want to imitate them. Some visitors from abroad will have positive feelings toward most of the Americans they meet. Others will not. Some will want to remain for a long time in the U.S.A. Others will want to go back home as soon as possible. People in both these groups will be more likely to benefit from their stays in the States if they understand the natives. "Understand" here means having a reasonably accurate set of ideas on the basis of which to interpret the behavior they see.

Let's look at an example, one that causes many foreigners to have negative feelings toward Americans.

Mohammad Abdullah is Egyptian. In his society, people place a high premium on family loyalty. Obligations to parents and siblings are an important part of daily life. Mohammad has come to the United States to earn a master's degree in civil engineering. Through the U.S. university he is attending he has a "host family," a local family that periodically invites him to their home for dinner or some other activity. The family's name is Wilson. Mr. Wilson is a 49-year-old engineer. His wife works half time in a lawyer's office. Their two children, a daughter who is 22 and a son who is 19, are both university students.

Mr. Wilson's father died two years ago. His mother, Mohammad learns, lives in a nursing home. One Sunday after having dinner with the Wilsons, Mohammad goes with them to visit Mr. Wilson's mother. The nursing home is full of frail, elderly people, most of whom are sitting silently in lounge areas or lying in their rooms. A few are playing cards or dominoes in the "game room" or are watching television. Mr. Wilson's mother is obviously old, but she can move around reasonably well and can carry on a normal conversation with anyone who talks a bit louder than usual. Mr. Wilson says he visits his mother once a week if at all possible. Sometimes he has to go out of town, so two weeks will pass between visits. His wife sometimes goes along on these visits; the children rarely do, since they are busy with their studies.

Mohammad is horrified. How can Mr. Wilson, who otherwise seems like a pleasant and generous person, stand to have his mother living in such a place? Why doesn't she live with Mr. Wilson?

How can Mohammad interpret Mr. Wilson's behavior? There are several possibilities: Mr. Wilson is a selfish, irresponsible person who does not understand the obligations children have toward their parents; or Mr. Wilson's mother has some medical or psychological problem that is not evident to him and that requires special care she could not get in Mr. Wilson's home; or Mr. Wilson's wife is a domineering woman who, for selfish reasons, refuses to have her husband's mother living in her house.

Any of these interpretations might be correct, but there are others that are more likely to explain the situation Mohammad has seen. If Mohammad understood the way in which Americans are trained to behave as independent, self-reliant individuals, he would be more likely to understand why Mr. Wilson's mother was in the nursing home. He would be more likely to realize that the mother might actually prefer to be in the nursing home rather than "be a burden" to her son and his family. Mohammad might understand, at least to some degree, the concern for "privacy" that leads Americans to keep to themselves in ways people in his own country would rarely do.

If Mohammad misinterpreted this situation he might well become unfriendly and even hostile to Mr. Wilson and his wife. His host family relationship would end. He would then lose a good opportunity to socialize, to meet Americans in age groups other than that of his fellow students, and to learn something through Mr. Wilson about the engineering profession as it is practiced in the United States.

If, on the other hand, Mohammad understood the factors underlying the nursing home situation in the same way the Wilsons probably do, he might go on to develop a closer and more rewarding relationship with the Wilson family.

So, understanding the natives can be beneficial. Misunderstanding them can eliminate opportunities and produce negative feelings that are inappropriate or unwarranted. This book can help foreign visitors understand Americans and thereby better achieve their own goals while in the United States.

HOW MUCH GENERALIZING IS ACCEPTABLE?

Who are these "Americans" we have been talking about? The United States of America covers a land area of 3,618,770 square miles (9,408,802 sq. km.) and is inhabited by some 230,000,000 individuals. According to the 1980 census, population density ranges from 986.2 people per square mile (2,564 per sq. km.) in the state of New Jersey to 0.7 per square mile (1.82

per sq. km.) in the state of Alaska. There are deserts, plains, marshlands, tundra, forests, and snow-covered mountains.

America's population reflects remarkable ethnic diversity. More than 20 per cent of the population of two major cities, Los Angeles and New York, were born in another country. In some other major cities (including San Francisco and Chicago) more than one of every ten residents is foreign-born. Non-white people outnumber whites in several large cities. Newspapers commonly use such terms as "Asian-American," "Italian-American," and "Arab-American" to reflect the persistence of various ethnic heritages within the United States. There are people whose skin is labeled white, black, brown, yellow, and red.

America's population includes Catholics, Protestants of many denominations, Jews of several persuasions, Moslems, Buddhists, animists, and people who believe in no supreme being or higher power. There are people who have many years of formal education and people who have nearly none. There are the very rich as well as the very poor. There are Republicans, Democrats, independents, socialists, Communists, libertarians, and adherents of other political views as well. There are lawyers, farmers, plumbers, teachers, social workers, immigration officers, and people in thousands of other occupations. Some live in urban areas and some in rural ones.

Given all this diversity, can one usefully talk about "Americans"? Probably so, if one is careful. Consider it this way:

In some ways, all people are alike.

In some ways, groups of people resemble each other.

In some ways, every person is unique.

In some ways, all people are alike. Anatomists and physiologists study ways in which the structure and functions of the human body operate, regardless of race, religion, income, or political opinion. A human pancreatic gland knows no political persuasion.

On the other hand, there are ways in which each person is unique. Psychologists study the manner in which each person's characteristics and experiences give rise to their particular attitudes and behavior.

In still other ways, groups of people resemble each other. One can find common characteristics among such groups as physicists, mothers, olympic athletes, and poor people. One can also find common characteristics among nationality groups—Americans, Nigerians, Irish, Egyptians, and so on. Members of these nationality groups have certain common experiences that result in similarities among them—even if, like many Americans, they do not recognize those similarities themselves. Americans might all seem different from each other until you compare them as a group to the Japanese (for example). Then it becomes clear that certain attitudes and behaviors are much more characteristic of the Americans while others are far more typical of the Japanese.

The predominant ideas, values, and behaviors of "Americans" are those of the white, middle class. People in that category have long held the large majority of the country's most influential positions. They have been the political and business leaders, the university presidents, scientists, journalists, and novelists who have successfully exerted influence on the society. So "American culture" as talked about in this book is the culture of the white, middle class.

Of course, not all Americans are white or middle class. But the society's main ideals have been forged by that group. Members of other groups usually (not always) agree with those ideals, at least on some level. Foreign visitors can find Americans who actively oppose the ideas that generally define the culture of their countrymen. "Hippie values," as cross-cultural training specialist Robert Kohls labels the countercultural ideas promoted by many young people in the 1960s, are very different from those of the white middle class. But hippie values are held by only a small minority of the population.

Generalizations are subject to exception and refinement. Readers of this book ought not to believe that, having read the book, they will understand all Americans. They will not. At best, they will have the beginning of an understanding of some aspects of some Americans. Readers are advised to go away from this book with minds that are still open to new observations and new interpretations.

ON ASKING "WHY?"

This is not a philosophical or political book. It is more of a practical guide. It barely concerns itself with the question of *why* Americans act as they do. There is a great temptation among people who encounter cultural differences to ask why those differences exist. "Why do they talk so loud?" "Why do men wear those narrow pieces of cloth tied up around their necks?" "Why are they so hard to get to know?" "Why do they smile and act so friendly when they can't even remember my name?" And countless other such questions, most of them ultimately unanswerable. The fact is that people do what they do. The "whys"—the reasons—are probably not determinable. The general characteristics of American culture have been ascribed by various observers to such factors as its 19th-century history as a large country with an open frontier to the west; its people's origins among dissenters and the lower classes in Europe; its high level of technological development; the influence of Christianity; the declining influence of Christianity; and its capitalist economic system. No one can say which of these explanations, or others, is "right." And it is not necessary, in daily dealings with Americans, to understand *why* they act as they do. So this book does not examine that topic in depth.

The assumption underlying this book's discussion of American and other cultures is that, as one well-known student of cross-cultural matters put it, "People act the way they were taught to act, and they all have different teachers." There *are* reasons for people's behaving the way they do, even if it is impossible to be certain what those reasons are. People who have grown up in the United States have been taught, or trained, to act in certain ways and not in others. They share a "culture." We will begin exploring that culture after a few words about Americans' conceptions of themselves and their attitudes toward foreigners.

HOW AMERICANS SEE THEMSELVES

It is usually helpful, when trying to understand others, to understand how they see themselves. A few comments about Americans' self-perceptions appear here; others come later.

Americans do not usually see themselves, when they are in the United States, as representatives of their country. They see themselves as individuals (we will stress this point later) who are different from all other individuals, whether those others are Americans or foreigners. Americans may say they have no culture, since they often conceive of culture as an overlay of arbitrary customs to be found only in other countries. Individual Americans may think they chose their own values, rather than having had their values and the assumptions on which they are based imposed on them by the society in which they were born. If you ask them to tell you something about "American culture," they may be unable to answer and they may even deny that there *is* an "American culture."

Because they think they are responsible as individuals for having chosen their basic values and their way of life, many Americans resent generalizations others make about them. Generalizations such as the ones in this book disturb many Americans. They may be offended by the notion that they hold certain ideas and behave in certain ways simply because they were born and raised in the United States, and not because they had consciously thought about those ideas and behaviors and chosen the ones they preferred.

At the same time, Americans will readily generalize about various subgroups within their own country. Northerners have stereotypes (that is, generalized, simplified notions) about Southerners, and vice versa. There are stereotypes of people from the country and people from the city; people from the coasts and people from inland; people from the Midwest; minority ethnic groups; minority religious groups; Texans; New Yorkers; Californians; Iowans; and so on. We will comment later on differences among these various groups of Americans. The point here is to realize that Americans see few generalizations that can safely be made about them, in part because they are "so individualistic" and in part because they think regional and other kinds of differences clearly distinguish Americans of various groups from each other.

HOW AMERICANS SEE FOREIGNERS

Like people everywhere else, Americans as they grow up are taught certain attitudes toward other countries and the people who live in them. Parents, teachers, school books, and the media are principal sources of information and attitudes about foreigners and foreign countries.

Americans generally believe that theirs is a superior country, probably the "greatest" country in the world. It is economically and militarily powerful; its influence extends to all parts of the globe. Americans generally believe their "democratic" political system is the best possible one, since it gives all citizens the right and opportunity to try to influence government policy, and since it protects citizens from arbitrary government actions. They also believe the system is superior because it gives them the freedom to complain about anything they consider wrong with it.

Americans generally believe their country's "free enterprise" economic system has enabled them to enjoy one of the highest standards of living in the history of the world.

If Americans consider their country to be superior, then it cannot be surprising that they often consider other countries to be inferior. The people in those other countries are assumed not to be quite as intelligent or hard-working or sensible as Americans are. Political systems in other countries are often assumed to be inadequately responsive to the public and excessively tolerant of corruption and abuse; other economic systems are regarded as less efficient than the American economic system. Foreigners (with the exception of Canadians and northern Europeans, who are generally viewed with respect) tend to be perceived as "underdeveloped Americans," prevented by their primitive economic and social systems and by their quaint cultural customs from achieving what they could if they were

Americans. Americans tend to suppose that people born in other countries are less fortunate than they are, and that most foreigners would prefer to live in the United States. The fact that millions of foreigners seek to enter or remain in the United States illegally every year supports this view. (The fact that billions of foreigners do not seek entry is ignored or discounted.)

Foreign visitors often find that Americans in general condescend to them, treating them a bit (or very much) like children who have limited experience and perhaps limited intelligence. Foreign visitors are well advised to remember that it is not malice or intentional ignorance that leads so many Americans to treat them like inferior beings. The Americans are, once again, acting the way they have been taught to act. They have been taught that they are superior, and they have learned the lesson.

There are obviously many exceptions to the preceding generalizations. The main exceptions are those Americans who have lived or at least traveled extensively in other countries and those who have in some other way had extensive experience with people from abroad. Many Americans will also make an exception for a foreigner who has demonstrated some skill, personality trait, or intellectual capability that commands respect. British writers, German scientists, Korean martial arts specialists, and Kenyan runners readily have many Americans' respect.

ON DESCRIBING AMERICANS

If you ask a Turk (for example) who is visiting the United States whether the Americans sh̄ ̄ has met think and act the way Turks normally do, she'll prob. bly say, without any hesitation, "No!" If you then ask her to explain *how* the Americans differ from the Turks, she will not answer so quickly. "Well, that's hard to say."

It is indeed difficult to explain how one cultural group differs from another. Anthropologists, sociologists, journalists, politicians, and others have tried various approaches to explaining the distinctive features of different cultures. There is no single best way to proceed.

This book's approach to helping foreign visitors understand Americans is divided into three parts. Part I presents some general ideas ("theory") about cultural differences and American culture as it compares to others. Part II gives information about specific aspects of American life, including friendships, social relationships, politics, religion, the media, and others. Part III offers guidelines for responding constructively to cultural differences.

PART I

★ ★ ★

General Ideas
about American Culture

How does American culture differ from others? There are several ways to address that question. The first way we will use, in Chapter One, is to consider the values and assumptions that Americans live by. The second is to examine their "communicative style." That we do in Chapter Two. Chapter Three is about the way in which Americans tend to think about things. Chapter Four, the last in Part I, has to do with American customs.

CHAPTER 1

☆ ☆ ☆

American Values and Assumptions

As people grow up, they learn certain values and assumptions from their parents and other relatives, their teachers, their books, newspapers, and television programs. "Values" are ideas about what is right and wrong, desirable and undesirable, normal and abnormal, proper and improper. In some cultures, for example, people are taught that men and women should inhabit separate social worlds, with some activities clearly in the men's domain and others clearly in the women's. In other cultures that value is not taught, or at least not widely. Men and women are considered to have more or less equal access to most roles in the society.

"Assumptions," as the term is used here, are the postulates, the unquestioned givens, about people, life, and "the way things are." (Scholars debate about the definition of such terms as "values," "assumptions," and others that appear in this book. But this book is not for scholars. It is for foreign visitors who want some basic understanding of America. Those visitors who want to read more scholarly works on the issues raised here can refer to the bibliography at the end of this book.) People in some societies assume, for example, that education takes place most efficiently when respectful young people absorb all they can of what older, wiser people already know. The young people do not challenge or even discuss what they are taught. The assumption is that learners are seeking *wisdom*, which comes with age. Young and inexperienced people are not wise enough to know what is worth discussing.

People in other societies assume that education requires learners to question and challenge the older "expert" when the

3

expert's ideas disagree with the learner's. The assumption is that learners are seeking *knowledge*, which a person can obtain regardless of age or social standing.

People who grow up in a particular culture share certain values and assumptions. That does not mean they all share exactly the same values to exactly the same extent; it does mean that most of them, most of the time, agree with each others' ideas about what is right and wrong, desirable and undesirable, and so on. They also agree, mostly, with each other's assumptions about human nature, social relationships, and so on.

Any list of values and assumptions is arbitrary. Depending on how one defines and categorizes things, one could make a three-item list of a country's major values and assumptions or a 30-item one. The list offered below has eight entries, each covering a set of closely related ideas.

Notice that these values and assumptions overlap with and support each other. In general, they agree with each other. They fit together. A culture can be viewed as a collection of values and assumptions that go together to shape the way a group of people perceive and relate to the world around them.

INDIVIDUALISM AND PRIVACY

The most important thing to understand about Americans is probably their devotion to "individualism." They have been trained since very early in their lives to consider themselves as separate individuals who are responsible for their own situations in life and their own destinies. They have not been trained to see themselves as members of a close-knit, tightly interdependent family, religious group, tribe, nation, or other collectivity.

You can see it in the way Americans treat their children. Even very young children are given opportunities to make their own choices and express their opinions. A parent will ask a one-year-old child what color balloon she wants, which candy bar she would prefer, or whether she wants to sit next to mommy or daddy. The child's preference will normally be accommodated.

Through this process, Americans come to see themselves as separate human beings who have their own opinions and who are responsible for their own decisions.

Indeed, American child-rearing manuals (such as Dr. Benjamin Spock's famous *Child and Baby Care*) state that the parents' objective in raising a child is to create a responsible, self-reliant individual who, by the age of 18 or so, is ready to move out of the parents' house and make his or her own way in life. Americans take this advice very seriously, so much so that a person beyond the age of about 20 who is still living at home with his or her parents may be thought to be "immature," "tied to the mother's apron strings," or otherwise unable to lead a normal, independent life.

Margaret Wohlenberg was the only American student among about 900 Malays enrolled at Indiana University's branch campus in Shah Alam, Malaysia, in 1986. She took Psychology 101, an introductory psychology course from the Indiana University curriculum, and earned a grade of A+. The other students' grades were lower. After the experience she reported:

> I do not think that Psych 101 is considered a very difficult course for the average freshman on the Bloomington campus [Indiana University's main location] but it is a great challenge to these [Malay] kids who have very little, if any, exposure to the concepts of Western psychology. . . . The American [while growing up] is surrounded, maybe even bombarded, by the propaganda of self-fulfillment and self-identity. Self-improvement and self-help—doing my own thing—seem at the core of American ideology.

But these are "quite unfamiliar ideas to the Malay students," Ms. Wohlenberg says. The Malay students' upbringing emphasizes the importance of family relationships and individual subservience to the family and the community.

Americans are trained to conceive of themselves as separate individuals, and they assume everyone else in the world is too. When they encounter a person from abroad who seems to them excessively concerned with the opinions of parents, with following traditions, or with fulfilling obligations to others, they assume that the person feels trapped or is weak, indecisive, or "overly dependent." They assume all people must resent being in situations where they are not "free to make up their own minds." They assume, furthermore, that after living for a time in the United States people will come to feel liberated from constraints arising outside themselves and will be grateful for the opportunity to "do their own thing" and "have it their own way."

It is this concept of themselves as individual decision-makers that blinds at least some Americans to the fact that they share a culture with each other. They have the idea, as mentioned above, that they have independently made up their own minds about the values and assumptions they hold. The notion that social factors outside themselves have made them "just like everyone else" in important ways offends their sense of dignity.

Americans, then, consider the ideal person to be an individualistic, self-reliant, independent person. They assume, incorrectly, that people from elsewhere share this value and this self-concept. In the degree to which they glorify "the individual" who stands alone and makes his or her own decisions, Americans are quite distinctive.

The individual that Americans idealize prefers an atmosphere of *freedom*, where neither the government nor any other external force or agency dictates what the individual does. For Americans, the idea of individual freedom has strong, positive connotations.

By contrast, people from many other cultures regard some of the behavior Americans legitimize by the label "individual freedom" to be self-centered and lacking in consideration for others. Mr. Wilson and his mother are good American individualists, living their own lives and interfering as little as possible with others. Mohammad Abdullah found their behavior almost immoral.

Foreigners who understand the degree to which Americans are imbued with the notion that the free, self-reliant individual is the ideal kind of human being will be able to understand many aspects of American behavior and thinking that otherwise might not make sense. A very few of the many possible examples:

Americans see as heroes those individuals who "stand out from the crowd" by doing something first, longest, most often, or otherwise "best." Examples are aviators Charles Lindberg and Amelia Earhart.

Americans admire people who have overcome adverse circumstances (for example, poverty or a physical handicap) and "succeeded" in life. Black educator Booker T. Washington is one example; the blind and deaf author and lecturer Helen Keller is another.

Many Americans do not display the degree of respect for their parents that people in more traditional or family-oriented societies commonly display. They have the conception that it was a sort of historical or biological accident that put them in the hands of particular parents, that the parents fulfilled their responsibilities to the children while the children were young, and now that the children have reached "the age of independence" the close child-parent tie is loosened, if not broken.

It is not unusual for Americans who are beyond the age of about 22 and who are still living with their parents to pay their parents for room and board. Elderly parents living with their grown children may do likewise. Paying for room and board is a way of showing independence, self-reliance, and responsibility for oneself.

Certain phrases one commonly hears among Americans capture their devotion to individualism: "Do your own thing." "I did it my way." "You'll have to decide that for yourself." "You made your bed, now lie in it." "If you don't look out for yourself, no one else will." "Look out for number one."

Closely associated with the value they place on individualism is the importance Americans assign to *privacy*. Americans assume that people "need some time to themselves" or "some time alone" to think about things or recover their spent psychological energy. Americans have great difficulty understanding foreigners who always want to be with another person, who dislike being alone.

If the parents can afford it, each child will have his or her own bedroom. Having one's own bedroom, even as an infant, inculcates in a person the notion that she is entitled to a place of her own where she can be by herself and—notice—keep her possessions. She will have *her* clothes, *her* toys, *her* books, and so on. These things will be hers and no one else's.

Americans assume that people have their "private thoughts" that might never be shared with anyone. Doctors, lawyers, psychiatrists, and others have rules governing "confidentiality" that are intended to prevent information about their clients' personal situations from becoming known to others.

Americans' attitudes about privacy can be difficult for foreigners to understand. Americans' houses, yards, and even their offices can seem open and inviting, yet, in the Americans' minds, there are boundaries that other people are simply not supposed to cross. When the boundaries are crossed, the Americans' bodies will visibly stiffen and their manner will become cool and aloof.

EQUALITY

Americans are also distinctive in the degree to which they believe in the ideal, as stated in their Declaration of Independence, that "all men are created equal." Although they sometimes violate the ideal in their daily lives, particularly in matters of interracial relationships, Americans have a deep faith that in some fundamental way all people (at least all American people) are of equal value, that no one is born superior to anyone else. "One man, one vote," they say, conveying the idea that any person's opinion is as valid and worthy of attention as any other person's opinion.

Americans are generally quite uncomfortable when someone treats them with obvious deference. They dislike being the subjects of open displays of respect—being bowed to, being deferred to, being treated as though they could do no wrong or make no unreasonable requests.

It is not just males who are created equal, in the American conception, but females too. While Americans often violate the idea in practice, they do generally assume that women are the equal of men, deserving of the same level of respect. Women, according to the viewpoint of the feminists who since the 1970s have been struggling to get what they consider a "fair shake" for females in the society, may be different from men but are in no way inferior to them.

This is not to say that Americans make no distinctions among themselves as a result of such factors as sex, age, wealth, or social position. They do. But the distinctions are acknowledged in subtle ways. Tone of voice, order of speaking, choice of words, seating arrangements—such are the means by which Americans acknowledge status differences among themselves. People of higher status are more likely to speak first, louder, and longer. They sit at the head of the table, or in the most comfortable chair. They feel free to interrupt other speakers more than others feel free to interrupt them. The higher status person may put a hand on the shoulder of the lower status person; if there is touching between the people involved, the higher status person will touch first.

Foreigners who are accustomed to more obvious displays of respect (such as bowing, averting eyes from the face of the higher status person, or using honorific titles) often overlook the ways in which Americans show respect for people of higher status. They think, incorrectly, that Americans are generally unaware of status differences and disrespectful of other people. What is distinctive about the American outlook on the matter of equality are the underlying assumptions that no matter what his or her initial station in life, any individual has the potential to achieve high standing and that everyone, no matter how unfortunate, deserves some basic level of respectful treatment.

INFORMALITY

Their notions of equality lead Americans to be quite *informal* in their general behavior and in their relationships with other people. Store clerks and waiters, for example, may introduce themselves by their first (given) names and treat customers in a casual, friendly manner. American clerks, like other Americans, have been trained to believe that they are as valuable as any other people, even if they happen to be engaged at a given time in an occupation that others might consider lowly. This informal behavior can outrage foreign visitors who hold high stations in countries where it is not assumed that "all men are created equal."

People from societies where general behavior is more formal than it is in America are struck by the informality of American speech, dress, and postures. Idiomatic speech (commonly called "slang") is heavily used on most occasions, with formal speech reserved for public events and fairly formal situations. People of almost any station in life can be seen in public wearing jeans, sandals, or other informal attire. People slouch down in chairs or lean on walls or furniture when they talk, rather than maintaining an erect bearing.

A brochure advertising a highly-regarded liberal-arts college contains a photograph showing the college's president, dressed in shorts and an old T-shirt, jogging past one of the classroom buildings on his campus. Americans are likely to find the photograph appealing: "Here is a college president who's just like anyone else. He doesn't think he's too good for us."

The superficial *friendliness* for which Americans are so well known is related to their informal, egalitarian approach to other people. "Hi!" they will say to just about anyone. "Howya doin?" (That is, "How are you doing?" or "How are you?") This behavior reflects less a special interest in the person addressed than a concern (not conscious) for showing that one is a "regular guy," part of a group of normal, pleasant people—like the college president.

More ideas about American notions of friendship will be discussed later.

THE FUTURE, CHANGE, AND PROGRESS

Americans are generally less concerned about history and traditions than are people from older societies. "History doesn't matter," many of them will say. "It's the future that counts." They look ahead. They have the idea that what happens in the future is within their control, or at least subject to their influence. They believe that the mature, sensible person sets goals for the future and works systematically toward them. They believe that people, as individuals or working cooperatively together, can change most aspects of the physical and social environment if they decide to do so, make appropriate plans, and get to work. Changes will presumably produce improvements. New things are better than old ones.

The long-time slogans of two major American corporations capture the Americans' assumptions about the future and about change. A maker of electrical appliances ended its radio and television commercials with the slogan, "Progress is our most important product." A huge chemical company that manufactured, among many other things, various plastics and synthetic fabrics, had this slogan: "Better things for better living through chemistry."

Closely associated with their assumption that they can bring about desirable changes in the future is the Americans' assumption that their physical and social environments are subject to human domination or control. Early Americans cleared forests, drained swamps, and altered the course of rivers in order to "build" the country. Contemporary Americans have gone to the moon in part just to prove they could do so.

This fundamental American belief in progress and a better future contrasts sharply with the fatalistic (Americans are likely to use that term with a negative or critical connotation) attitude that characterizes people from many other cultures, notably Latin, Asian, and Arab, where there is a pronounced reverence for the past. In those cultures the future is considered to be in the hands of "fate," "God," or at least the few powerful people or families that dominate the society. The idea that they could somehow shape their own futures seems naive or even arrogant.

Americans are generally impatient with people they see as passively accepting conditions that are less than desirable. "Why don't they do something about it?" Americans will ask. Americans don't realize that a large portion of the world's population sees the world around them as something they cannot change, but rather as something to which they must submit, or at least something with which they must seek to live in harmony.

GOODNESS OF HUMANITY

The future cannot be better if people in general are not fundamentally good and improvable. Americans assume that human nature is basically good, not basically evil. Foreign visitors will see them doing many things that are based on the assumption that people are good and can make themselves better. Some examples:

Getting more education or training. Formal education is not just for young people, but for everyone. Educational institutions offer "extension classes," night classes, correspondence courses, and television courses so that people who have full-time jobs or who live far from a college or university have the opportunity to get more education. Many post-secondary students are adults who seek to "improve themselves" by learning more.

"Non-formal" educational opportunities in the form of "workshops," seminars, or training programs are widely available. Through them people can learn about a huge array of topics, from being a better parent to investing money more wisely to behaving more assertively.

Rehabilitation. Except in extreme cases where it would clearly be futile, efforts are made to rehabilitate people who have lost some physical capacity as a result of injury or illness. A person who "learned to walk again" after a debilitating accident is widely admired.

Rehabilitation is not just for the physically infirm, but for those who have failed socially as well. Jails, prisons, and detention centers are intended as much to train inmates to be socially useful as they are to punish them. A widespread (but not universally-held) assumption is that people who violate the law do so more because of adverse environmental conditions such as poverty than because they themselves are evil individuals.

Belief in democratic government. We have already discussed some of the assumptions that underlie the American
belief that a democratic form of government is best—assumptions about individualism, freedom, and equality. Another assumption is that people can make life better for themselves and
others through the actions of governments they choose.

Voluntarism. It is not just through the actions of government or other formal bodies that life can be improved, but
through the actions of citizen volunteers as well. Many foreign
visitors are awed by the array of activities Americans support
on a voluntary basis: parent-teacher organizations in elementary and secondary schools, community "service clubs" that
raise money for worthy causes, organizations of families that
play host to foreign students, "clean-up, paint-up, fix-up" campaigns to beautify communities, organizations working to pre-
serve wilderness areas, and on and on.

Educational campaigns. When Americans perceive a social problem they are likely (often on a voluntary basis) to
establish an "educational campaign" to "make the public
aware" of the dangers of something and induce people to take
preventative or corrective action. Thus there are campaigns
concerning smoking, drugs, alcohol, child abuse, and many
specific diseases.

Self-improvement. Americans assume themselves to be
improvable. We have already mentioned their participation in
various educational and training programs. Mention should
also be made of the array of "how-to" books Americans buy, and
the number of group activities they join in order to make themselves "better." Through things they read or groups they join
Americans can stop smoking, stop using alcohol, lose weight,
get into better physical condition, manage their time more
effectively, manage their money more effectively, become better at their jobs, and improve themselves in countless other
ways.

"Where there's a will, there's a way," the Americans say.
People who want to make things better can do so if only they
have a strong enough motivation.

TIME

For Americans, time is a "resource" that, like water or coal, can be used well or poorly. "Time is money," they say. "You only get so much time in this life; you'd best use it wisely." The future will not be better than the past or the present, as Americans are trained to see things, unless people use their time for constructive, future-oriented activities. Thus, Americans admire a "well-organized" person, one who has a written list of things to do and a schedule for doing them. The ideal person is punctual (that is, arrives at the scheduled time for a meeting or event) and is considerate of other people's time (that is, does not "waste people's time" with conversation or other activity that has no visible, beneficial outcome).

The American attitude toward time is not necessarily shared by others, especially non-Europeans. They are more likely to conceive of time as something that is simply there around them, not something they can "use." One of the more difficult things many foreign businessmen and students must adjust to in the States is the notion that time must be saved whenever possible and used wisely every day.

In their efforts to use their time wisely, Americans are sometimes seen by foreign visitors as automatons, unhuman creatures who are so tied to their clocks and their schedules that they cannot participate in or enjoy the human interactions that are the truly important things in life. "They are like little machines running around," one foreign visitor said.

The premium Americans place on *efficiency* is closely related to their concepts of the future, change, and time. To do something efficiently is to do it in the way that is quickest and requires the smallest expenditure of resources. American businesses sometimes hire "efficiency experts" to review their operations and suggest ways in which they could accomplish more than they are currently accomplishing with the resources they are investing. Popular periodicals carry suggestions for more efficient ways to shop, cook, clean house, do errands, raise children, tend the yard, and on and on.

In this context the "fast-food industry" can be seen as a clear example of an American cultural product. McDonald's,

Kentucky Fried Chicken, Pizza Hut, and other fast-food establishments prosper in a country where many people want to minimize the amount of time they spend preparing and eating meals. The millions of Americans who take their meals at fast-food restaurants cannot have much interest in lingering over their food while conversing with friends, as millions of Europeans do. As McDonald's restaurants have spread around the world, they have been viewed as symbols of American society and culture, bringing not just hamburgers but an emphasis on speed, efficiency, and shiny cleanliness. The typical American food, some observers argue, is fast food.

ACHIEVEMENT, ACTION, WORK, AND MATERIALISM

"He's a hard worker," one American might say in praise of another. Or, "She gets the job done." These expressions convey the typical American's admiration for a person who approaches a task conscientiously and persistently, seeing it through to a successful conclusion. More than that, these expressions convey an admiration for *achievers*, people whose lives are centered around efforts to accomplish some physical, measurable thing. Social psychologists use the term "achievement motivation" to describe what appears to be the intention underlying Americans' behavior. "Affiliation" is another kind of motivation, shown by people whose main intent seems to be to establish and retain a set of relationships with other people. The achievement motivation predominates in America.

Foreign visitors commonly remark that "Americans work harder than I expected them to." (Perhaps these visitors have been excessively influenced by American movies and television programs, which are less likely to show people working than to show them driving around in fast cars or pursuing members of the opposite sex.) While the so-called "Protestant work ethic" may have lost some of its hold on Americans, there is still a strong belief that the ideal person is a "hard worker." A hard worker is one who "gets right to work" on a task without delay, works efficiently, and completes the task in a way that meets reasonably high standards of quality.

Hard workers are admired not just on the job, but in other aspects of life as well. Housewives, students, and people volunteering their services to charitable organizations can also be "hard workers" who make "significant achievements."

More generally, Americans like *action*. They do indeed believe it is important to devote significant energy to their jobs or to other daily responsibilities. Beyond that, they tend to believe they should be *doing* something most of the time. They are usually not content, as people from many countries are, to sit for hours and talk with other people. They get restless and impatient. They believe they should be doing something, or at least making plans and arrangements for doing something later.

People without the Americans' action orientation often see Americans as frenzied, always "on the go," never satisfied, compulsively active. They may, beyond that, evaluate Americans negatively for being unable to relax and enjoy life's pleasures. Even recreation, for Americans, is often a matter of acquiring lavish equipment, making elaborate plans, then going somewhere to *do* something.

Americans tend to define people by the jobs they have. ("Who is he?" "He's the vice president in charge of personal loans at the bank.") Their family backgrounds, educational attainments, and other characteristics are considered less important in identifying people than the jobs they have.

There is usually a close relationship between the job a person has and the level of the person's income. Americans tend to measure a person's "success" in life by referring to the amount of money he has acquired. Being a bank vice president is quite respectable, but being a bank president is more so. The president gets a higher salary. So the president can buy more things—a bigger house and car, a boat, more neckties and shoes, and so on.

Americans are often criticized for being so "materialistic," so concerned with acquiring possessions. For Americans, though, this materialism is natural and proper. They have been taught that it is a good thing to achieve—to work hard, acquire more material badges of their success, and in the process assure a better future for themselves and their immediate families. And, like people from elsewhere, they do what they are taught.

DIRECTNESS AND ASSERTIVENESS

Americans, as has been said before, generally consider themselves to be frank, open, and direct in their dealings with other people. "Let's lay our cards on the table," they say. Or, "Let's stop playing games and get to the point." These and many other common phrases convey the Americans' idea that people should explicitly state what they think and what they want from other people.

Americans tend to assume that conflicts or disagreements are best settled by means of forthright discussions among the people involved. If I dislike something you are doing, I should tell you about it directly so you will know, clearly and from me personally, how I feel about it. Bringing in other people to mediate a dispute is considered somewhat cowardly, the act of a person without enough courage to speak directly to someone else.

The word "assertive" is the adjective Americans commonly use to describe the person who plainly and directly expresses feelings and requests. People who are inadequately assertive can take "assertiveness training classes."

Americans will often speak openly and directly to others about things they dislike. They will try to do so in a manner they call "constructive," that is, a manner which the other person will not find offensive or unacceptable. If they do not speak openly about what is on their minds, they will often convey their reactions in nonverbal ways (without words, but through facial expressions, body positions, and gestures). Americans are not taught, as people in many Asian countries are, that they should mask their emotional responses. Their words, the tone of their voices, or their facial expressions will usually reveal when they are feeling angry, unhappy, confused, or happy and content. They do not think it improper to display these feelings, at least within limits. Many Asians feel embar-

rassed around Americans who are exhibiting a strong emotional response to something. (On the other hand, as we shall see
later, Latins and Arabs are generally inclined to display their
emotions more openly than Americans do, and to view Americans as unemotional and "cold.")

But Americans are often less direct and open than they
realize. There are in fact many restrictions on their willingness
to discuss things openly. It is difficult to categorize those restrictions, and the restrictions are often not "logical" in the
sense of being consistent with each other. Generally, though,
Americans are reluctant to speak openly when:

the topic is in an area they consider excessively personal, such
as unpleasant body or mouth odors, sexual functioning, or personal inadequacies;

they want to say "no" to a request that has been made of them
but do not want to offend or "hurt the feelings of" the person
who made the request;

they are not well enough acquainted with the other person to
be confident that direct discussion will be accepted in the constructive way that is intended; and, paradoxically,

they know the other person very well (it might be a spouse or
close friend) and they do not wish to risk giving offense and cre-
ating negative feelings by talking about some delicate problem.

A Chinese student invited an American couple to his
apartment to share a dinner he had prepared. They compli-
mented him warmly about the quality of his meal. "Several
Americans have told me they like my cooking," he replied, "but
I cannot tell whether they are sincere or just being polite. Do
you think they really like it?"

All of this is to say that Americans, even though they see
themselves as properly assertive and even though they often
behave in open and direct ways, have limits on their openness.
It is not unusual for them to try to avoid direct confrontations
with other people when they are not confident that the con-
frontation can be carried out in a "constructive" way that will

result in an acceptable compromise. (Americans' ideas about the benefits of compromise are discussed later.)

Foreigners often find themselves in situations where they are unsure of or even unaware of what the Americans around them are thinking or feeling and are unable to find out because the Americans will not tell them directly what they have in mind. Two examples:

Sometimes a person from another country will "smell bad" to Americans because he does not follow the same hygienic practices (daily bathing and use of deodorants) Americans tend to think are necessary (see Chapter Fifteen). But Americans will rarely tell a person (foreign or otherwise) that he has "body odor" because that topic is considered too sensitive.

A foreigner (or another American, for that matter) may ask a "favor" that an American considers inappropriate. She might ask to borrow a car, for example, or ask for help with an undertaking that will require more time than the American thinks she has available. The American will want to decline the request, but will fear saying "no" directly.

Americans might feel especially reluctant to say "no" directly to a foreigner, for fear of making the person feel unwelcome or discriminated against. They will often try to convey the "no" indirectly, by saying such things as "it's not convenient now" or by repeatedly postponing an agreed-upon time for doing something.

Despite these limitations, Americans are generally more direct and open than people from many other countries. They will not try to mask their emotions, as Scandinavians tend to do. They are much less concerned with "face" (that is, avoiding embarrassment to themselves or others) than most Asians are. To them, being "honest" is usually more important than preserving harmony in interpersonal relationships.

Americans use the words "pushy" or "aggressive" to describe a person who is excessively assertive in expressing opinions or making requests. The line between acceptable assertiveness and unacceptable aggressiveness is difficult to draw.

Iranians and people from other countries where forceful arguing and negotiating are common forms of interaction risk being
seen as aggressive or pushy when they treat Americans in the
way they treat people at home. This topic is elaborated upon in
Chapter Two.

CHAPTER 2

☆ ☆ ☆

The Communicative
Style of Americans

Pushy Greeks. Shy Chinese. Opinionated Germans. Emotional Mexicans, Brazilians, and Italians. Cold British. Loud Africans. These are among the stereotypes or general ideas Americans have about some other nationalities. In part, these stereotypes arise from differences in what the communications scholar Dean Barnlund calls "communicative style."

When people talk to each other, they exhibit a communicative style that is strongly influenced by their culture. Communicative style refers to several characteristics of conversations between individuals, according to Barnlund. Communicative style refers to (1) the topics people prefer to discuss, (2) their favorite forms of interaction in conversation, (3) the depth to which they want to get involved with each other, (4) the communication channels (verbal or nonverbal) on which they rely, and (5) the level of meaning ("factual" vs. "emotional") to which they are most attuned.

Naturally, people prefer to use their own communicative style. Issues about communicative style rarely arise when two people from the same culture are together because their styles generally agree. Most people—including most Americans—are as unaware of their communicative style as they are of their basic values and assumptions. Foreigners who understand something about the Americans' communicative style will be less likely to misinterpret or misjudge Americans than will foreigners who don't know the common characteristics of interpersonal communication among Americans. They will also have a better understanding of some of the stereotypes Americans have about other nationality groups.

21

PREFERRED DISCUSSION TOPICS

When they first encounter another person, Americans engage in a kind of conversation they call "small talk." The most common topic of small talk is the weather; another very common topic is the speakers' current physical surroundings—the room or building they are in, the sidewalk where they are standing, or whatever is appropriate. Later, after the preliminaries, Americans may talk about past experiences they have both had, such as watching a particular TV program, going to New York, or eating at a particular restaurant.

Beyond these very general topics of small talk, there is variation according to the life situation of the people involved and the setting in which the conversation is taking place. Students are likely to talk about their teachers and classes; if they are of the same sex, they are likely to discuss their social lives. Adults may discuss their jobs, recreational interests, houses, or family matters. Men are likely to talk about sports or cars. Housewives, whose numbers are steadily decreasing in American society, are likely to talk about their children, if they have any, or about household matters or personal care (e.g., hairdos).

Americans are explicitly taught not to discuss religion and politics unless they are fairly well acquainted with the people they are talking to. (In public meetings Americans will openly debate about political matters, but we are talking here about communicative style in interpersonal situations.) Politics and religion are thought to be "controversial," and discussing a controversial topic can lead to an argument. Americans, as we will discuss under "Favorite Forms of Interaction," are taught to avoid arguments.

Unlike Americans, people from Germany, Iran, and many other countries consider politics, and sometimes religion as well, to be excellent topics for informal discussion and debate. For them, discussing—and arguing about—politics is a favorite way to pass the time.

There are other topics Americans generally avoid because they are "too personal." Financial matters is one. Inquiries about a person's earnings or about the amount someone paid for an item are usually beyond the bounds of acceptable topics. So are body and mouth odors (as already mentioned), the functioning of the urogenital organs, sexual behavior and responses, and fantasies.

Upon first meeting, people from Spanish-speaking countries may have long interchanges about the health and well-being of each other's family members. Saudis, by contrast, consider questions about family members inappropriate unless the people talking know each other well. Americans might inquire briefly about family members ("How's the wife?" or "How're the kids?"), but politeness in brief and casual encounters does not require dwelling on the subject.

As was already said, people prefer to use their own communicative styles. That means, among other things, they prefer to abide by their own ideas about conversation topics that are appropriate for any given setting. Foreigners who have different ideas from Americans about what topics are appropriate for a particular setting are very likely to feel uncomfortable when they are talking with Americans. They do not feel they can participate in the conversation on an equal footing. But the Americans resist (quite unconsciously) their attempts to bring up a different topic. ,

Listening to American small talk leads some foreigners to the erroneous conclusion that Americans are intellectually incapable of carrying on a discussion about anything significant. Some foreigners believe that topics more complex than weather, sports, or social lives are beyond the Americans' ability to comprehend.

FAVORITE FORMS OF INTERACTION

The typical conversation between Americans takes a form that can be called *repartee*. No one speaks for very long. Speakers take turns frequently, often after only a few sentences have been spoken. "Watching a conversation between two Americans is like watching a table tennis game," a British observer said. "Your head goes back and forth and back and forth so fast it almost makes your neck hurt."

Americans tend to be impatient with people who take long turns. Such people are said to "talk too much." Many Americans have difficulty paying attention to someone who speaks more than a few sentences at a time, as Nigerians, Arabs, and some others do. Americans admire conciseness, or what they call "getting to the point."

Americans engage in little *ritual* interaction. Only a few ritual interchanges are common: "How are you?" "I'm fine, thank you," "Nice to meet you," and "Hope to see you again." These things are said under certain circumstances Americans learn to recognize, and, like any ritual interchanges, are concerned more with form than with substance. That is, the questions are supposed to be asked and the statements are supposed to be made in particular circumstances, no matter what the people involved are feeling or what they really have in mind. In many Americans' opinions, people who rely heavily on ritual interchanges are "too shy" or "too polite," unwilling to reveal their true natures and ideas.

Americans are generally impatient with long ritual interchanges about family members' health—common among Latin Americans—or invocations of a supreme being's goodwill—common among Arabs—considering them a waste of time.

A third form of interaction, one Americans tend to avoid, is *argument*. Americans seem to suppose that an argument with another person might result in termination of their relationship. They do not conceive of argument as a sport or a pleasurable pastime. If Americans are in a discussion in which a difference of opinion is emerging, they are likely to say, "Let's not get into an argument about this." Rather than argue, they will prefer to find areas of agreement, change the topic, or even physically move away from the person they have been talking to. Not surprisingly, people who like to argue are likely to be labelled "pushy," "aggressive," or "opinionated."

If an argument is unavoidable, Americans believe it should be conducted in calm, moderate tones and with a minimum of gesturing. Loud voices, vigorous use of arms, more than one person talking at a time—to most Americans these are signs that a physical fight, or at least an unproductive "shouting match," might develop. They believe people should "stay cool" when presenting their viewpoints.

This is not to say that no Americans argue. Certainly there are those who do, even in interpersonal situations. Generally, though, they prefer not to. One result of their aversion to arguing is that they get little practice in verbally defending their viewpoints. And one result of that, in turn, is that they may appear less intelligent than they actually are.

A fourth and final form of interaction is *self-disclosure*. Conversations with a large amount of small talk (or of ritual interchange) usually produce little self-disclosure. That is, the people involved reveal little if anything about their personal lives or situations. What Americans regard as "personal" in this context is their feelings and their opinions about controversial matters. In most situations Americans reveal little that is personal. Women will disclose more about themselves to other women than they will to men and than men will to anyone. Of course, much more self-revelation takes place in the context of a close friendship.

Americans are probably not extreme with respect to the amount of self-disclosure that takes place in interpersonal encounters. Foreign visitors who are accustomed to more self-revelation may feel frustrated in their efforts to get to know Americans. Those accustomed to less self-disclosure may be embarrassed by some of the things Americans do talk about.

DEPTH OF INVOLVEMENT SOUGHT

Cultural backgrounds influence the degree to which people want to become closely connected with other people outside their families. People from some cultures are looking for close, interdependent relationships. They value commitment to other people and they want friendships in which there are virtually no limits to what the friends will do for each other.

Americans cause immense frustration for foreigners by their apparent inability to become closely involved with other people in the way the foreigners want and expect them to. "Americans just don't know how to be friends," many foreigners say. "You never feel that you are free to call on them at any time, or that they will help you no matter what."

Many Americans do have what they call close friends, with whom they discuss intimate personal concerns and to whom they feel special attachments and strong obligations. But such friendships are small in number. Much more numerous are relationships with people who might more accurately be called "acquaintances" than "friends." With acquaintances, the degree of intimate involvement and sense of mutual obligation is much lower. Americans are likely to use the term "friend" to cover a wide range of types of relationships, much to the confusion of visitors from abroad.

Americans tend to relate to each other as occupants of roles rather than as whole people. Another person might be a roommate, classmate, neighbor, colleague from work, weekend boater, or teacher. Certain behaviors are expected of people in each of those roles. All is well among Americans if people behave according to the generally-accepted notions of what is appropriate for the role in which they find themselves. Other aspects of their behavior are not considered relevant, as they are in a society where attention is paid to the "kind of person" one is dealing with. An accountant may be a chain-smoking, hard-drinking adulterer, but if he is a good accountant I am likely to use his services even if I disapprove of chain-smoking, heavy use of alchohol, and adultery. His personal life is not relevant to his ability as an accountant.

Americans often seem to fear close involvement with other people. They will avoid becoming dependent on others. They do not want others, with the possible exception of immediate family members, to be dependent on them. (Remember, they have been brought up to see the ideal person as independent and self-reliant.) They are likely to be extremely cautious when they meet a new person who seems to want to get closely involved with them. "What does this person want?" they seem to be asking. "How much of my time will it take? Will I be able to withdraw from the relationship if it gets too demanding?"

Foreigners will want to realize that Americans often have difficulty becoming "close friends" with each other, not just with unfamiliar people from other countries.

CHANNELS PREFERRED

Americans depend more on spoken words than on nonverbal behavior to convey their messages. They think it is important to be able to "speak up" and "say what's on your mind." They admire a person who has a moderately large vocabulary and who can express herself clearly and cleverly. But they distrust people who are, in their view, excessively articulate. A person with a very large vocabulary is likely to be considered "over-educated" or "a snob." A person who is extremely skillful at presenting verbal messages is usually suspect: "Is he trying to sell me something?" "What's he up to? He's a smooth talker, so you'd better watch him."

People from some other cultures, notably the Arabs, Iranians, and some (especially Southern) Europeans, prize verbal agility more than Americans do. People from those cultures, when they visit America, are likely to have two different reactions to Americans and their use of language. The first is to wonder why Americans seem suspicious of them. The second is to suppose that Americans, since they cannot carry on discussions (or arguments, as we have seen) very well, must not be very intelligent or well informed. "Americans are not as intelligent as we are," said an Iranian student who had been in the States for several years. "In all the time I've been here I've never heard one of them talk about anything more important than sports and the weather. They just don't know anything about politics and they don't understand it."

It is no doubt the case that the level of knowledge and understanding of political matters is lower in the States than it is in many other so-called advanced countries. It does not necessarily follow, though, that Americans are less intelligent than people elsewhere. To conclude from their relatively limited verbal abilities that they are unintelligent is to misperceive the situation.

Other people come to America from cultures where people generally talk less than Americans do and rely more on nonverbal means of understanding each other. Such people tend to find Americans "too loud," "too talkative," and not sensitive enough to understand other people without putting everything into words. "You Americans!" an exasperated Japanese woman said when she was pressed for details about an unpleasant situation involving a friend of hers. "You have to *say* everything!"

More ideas about the complex subject of nonverbal behavior are discussed in Chapter Twenty-One.

Americans' preference for verbal over nonverbal means of communicating pertains also to the written word. Words are important to Americans, and written words are often more important than ones that are merely spoken. Formal agreements, contracts, and decisions are normally written down. Official notices and advisories are written. "Put it in writing," the Americans say, if it is important and you want it to receive appropriate attention. Foreign students and businessmen sometimes get themselves into difficulty because they have not paid enough attention (by American standards) to written notices, procedures, or deadlines.

LEVEL OF MEANING EMPHASIZED

Americans generally pay more attention to the factual than to the emotional content of messages. They are uncomfortable with displays of more than moderate emotion, and they are taught in school to detect—and dismiss—"emotional appeals" in other people's statements or arguments. They are urged to "look for the facts" and "weigh the evidence" when they are in the process of making a judgment or decision.

While there are of course areas in which Americans are emotional or sentimental, they are generally a bit suspicious of a person whose main message is an emotional one. They generally overlook (unless it is so obvious that they cannot) the mood of the person they are talking to and listen for the "facts" in what the person has to say. Statements or arguments relying heavily on emotional appeals are not likely to be taken seriously.

More ideas on this topic can be found in the next chapter, which is on the closely-related subject of "American Patterns of Thinking."

Before going on, however, it is important to emphasize two

points that have been raised several times already. The first is that people naturally prefer to use their own communicative style. The second is that differences in communicative style can cause serious problems in intercultural interactions. They produce uneasiness, misjudgments, and misinterpretations whose source is not clear to the people involved. Americans, for example, believe they are acting "naturally" when they engage in small talk with a person they have just met. They do not expect to have their level of intelligence judged on the basis of their small talk. But if the person they just met is from a culture where conversations with new acquaintances "naturally" take some form other than small talk, then the person may well be evaluating the American's intellectual qualities. The result of all this is likely to be negative feelings and judgments on both sides. The stereotypes listed at the opening of this chapter arise at least in part from judgments made on the basis of differences in communicative style.

Foreigners who understand the American communicative style will be far less likely to contribute to these misunderstandings and negative feelings, and their opportunities for constructive interaction will be much greater.

CHAPTER 3

☆ ☆ ☆

Ways of Reasoning

To understand how Americans think about things, it is necessary to understand about "the point." Americans mention it often: "Let's get right to the point," they will say. "My point is. . . ." "What's the point of all this?"

The "point" is the idea or piece of information that Americans presume is, or should be, at the center of people's thinking, writings, and spoken comments. Speakers and writers are supposed to "make their points clear," meaning that they are supposed to say or write explicitly the idea or piece of information they wish to convey.

People from many other cultures have different ideas about the point. Africans traditionally recount stories that convey the thoughts they have in mind, rather than stating "the point" explicitly. Japanese traditionally speak indirectly, leaving the listener to figure out what the point is. Thus, while an American might say to a friend, "I don't think that coat goes very well with the rest of your outfit," a Japanese might say, "Maybe this other coat would look even better than the one you have on." Americans value a person who "gets right to the point." Japanese are likely to consider such a person insensitive if not rude.

The Chinese and Japanese languages are characterized by vagueness and ambiguity. The precision, directness, and clarity Americans associate with "the point" cannot be attained, at least not with any grace, in Chinese and Japanese. Speakers of those languages are thus compelled to learn a new way of reasoning and conveying their ideas if they are going to interact satisfactorily with Americans.

As these examples indicate, different cultures teach different ways of thinking about things, of gathering and weighing evidence, of presenting viewpoints and reaching conclusions. These differences are evident in discussions and arguments, public speeches, and written presentations.

It is not enough to make a point, according to the typical American notion. A responsible speaker or writer is also expected to prove that the point is true, accurate, or valid. As they grow up, Americans learn what is and is not acceptable as "proof." The most important element of a proof is "the facts." A student might state an opinion and the teacher will ask, "What are your facts?" Or, "What data do you have to support that?" The teacher is telling the student that without facts to support the opinion, the opinion will not be considered legitimate or valid.

Americans assume there are "facts" of life, of nature, and of the universe that can be discovered by trained people (usually called "scientists") using special techniques, equipment, and ways of thinking. "Scientific facts," as the Americans call them, are assumed to exist independently of any individual person who studies them or talks about them. This important assumption—that there are facts existing independently of the people who observe them—is not shared throughout the world.

The most reliable facts, in the American view, are those in the form of quantities—specific numbers, percentages, rates, rankings, or amounts. Many foreign visitors in the States are struck—if not stunned—by the quantity of numbers and statistics they encounter in the media and in daily conversations. "McDonald's has sold 8.7 billion hamburgers," say signs all over the country. "Nine out of ten doctors recommend this brand of mouthwash," says a radio announcer or a magazine advertisement. (Doctors are viewed as scientists or appliers of science, and are held in very high esteem.) "The humidity is at 27 per cent," says the television weather reporter. "The barometric pressure is at 29.32 and rising. Yesterday's high temperature in Juneau, Alaska, was 47 degrees."

Americans feel secure in the presence of all these numbers.

Foreign visitors often wonder what significance the numbers could possibly have.

Citing quantifiable facts is generally considered the best way to prove a point. Facts based on personal experience are also persuasive. Americans accept information and ideas that arise from their own experience or that of others they know and trust. Television advertisers seek to capitalize on this aspect of American reasoning through commercials that portray presumably average people (a woman in a kitchen, for example, or two men in an auto repair shop) testifying that in their experience the product or service being advertised is a good one. Other credible testifiers are people dressed to look like scientists or doctors and celebrities from the worlds of entertainment and athletics.

Of the various ways of having personal experience, Americans regard the sense of *sight* as the most reliable. "I saw it with my own eyes" means that it undoubtedly happened. In a court of law, an "eyewitness" is considered the most reliable source of information. If a speaker has failed to make his purpose in speaking clear, Americans will say, "I don't see the point."

Along with their trust in facts goes a distrust of emotions. School children are taught (but do not always learn) to disregard the emotional aspects of an argument as they look for "the facts." In their suspicion of emotional statements, Americans differ from many others. Iranians, for example, have a tradition of eloquent, emotion-filled speech. They quote revered poets who have captured the feeling they want to convey. They seek to move their audiences to accept them and their viewpoints not because of the facts they have presented but because of the human feelings they share.

A Brazilian graduate student was having difficulty in his English writing class. "It's not just a matter of verbs and nouns," he said. "My teacher tells me I'm too subjective. Too emotional. I must learn to write my points more clearly."

In evaluating the significance of a point or a proof, Americans are most likely to consider its practical usefulness. Americans are famous for their pragmatism, that is, their interest in whether a fact or idea has practical consequences. A good idea is a practical idea. Other adjectives that convey approval of ideas or information are "realistic," "down-to-earth," "hard-headed," and "sensible."

Americans tend to distrust theory and generalizations, which they might label "impractical," "unrealistic," "too abstract," "a lot of hot air," or "just theoretical." A Latin American graduate student, for example, heard himself being criticized (openly and directly) by the American professor in his international organization class. The student had written a paper concerning a particular international organization and had talked about the principles of national sovereignty, self-determination, and non-interference in the internal affairs of other countries. "That's just pure Latin American bunk," the professor said to him. "That's nothing but words and theory. It has nothing to do with what really happens." The embarrassed student was told to write another paper.

Latin Americans and many Europeans are likely to attach more weight to ideas and theories than Americans are. Rather than compiling facts and statistics on the basis of which to reach conclusions, they are likely to generalize from one theory to another, or from a theory to facts, according to certain rules of logic. A Soviet visitor in Detroit in the 1960s asked his hosts where the masses of unemployed workers were. His hosts said there were no masses of unemployed workers. "There must be," the visitor insisted. "Marx says the capitalist system produces massive unemployment among the workers. You must be hiding them somewhere."

For this visitor, "truth" came not from facts he observed, but from a theory he believed. Americans believe in some theories, of course, but in general they are suspicious of theory and generalizations and more at ease with specific facts.

In some Chinese traditions, truth and understanding come neither from accumulating facts nor generalizing from theories, but from silent meditation. In Zen, truths cannot even be expressed in language. Zen masters do not tell their students what the point is.

Another element of ways of reasoning, beyond considerations about facts and theory as ways of reaching or supporting conclusions, is the matter of cause-and-effect relationships. Americans tend to suppose that most events have some knowable, physical cause. "Things don't just happen," they often say. "Something makes them happen." Very few events are considered to result from "chance" or "luck" or "fate." Religious Americans will ascribe certain kinds of events (such as the otherwise inexplicable death of a child) to "God's will." But these intangible factors are not usually held responsible for what happens to people. As suggested in Chapter One, most Americans have difficulty even comprehending the notion, so prevalent in many other parts of the world, that "fate" deter-' mines what happens in people's lives.

When people with differing ways of reasoning are interacting, the typical feeling they both get is that the other person "just doesn't understand" and "isn't making sense." Each then tries harder to be more "logical," not realizing that the problem is their differing conceptions of what is logical. Foreigners in America will need to learn that Americans will consider them "not logical," "too emotional," or "fuzzy-minded" if they do not use specific facts to support or illustrate their ideas and opinions, if they speak mainly in terms of abstractions and generalizations, or if they attribute important events to non-material causes.

Foreign students have a particular need to learn how Americans think about things and how they organize their thoughts in speech and writing. Unless they do, they will have trouble writing papers or giving speeches that American audiences (including teachers) will take seriously.

CHAPTER 4

☆ ☆ ☆

Differences in Customs

The Japanese businessman, arms extending downwards from his shoulders, bowed from his waist toward the American businessman to whom he was just introduced. His eyes were directed ahead; his face showed no particular expression.

The American businessman stood erect. His eyes focused on the Japanese man's eyes. He smiled and put out his right hand.

Both men smiled briefly in embarrassment. The Japanese man straightened up and put out his right hand. The American withdrew his hand and bowed his head. A broader smile of embarrassment, and some noise from each man—not really words, just some sounds from their throats—indicating discomfort. They were in the midst of a clash of customs; they had different habits for greeting people they were being introduced to.

When people are planning to go to another country, they expect to encounter certain kinds of differences. They usually expect the weather and the food to be different. They expect to find differences in some of the material aspects of life, such as the availability of cars, electricity, and home heating systems. And, without knowing the details, they expect differences in customs. Customs are the behaviors that are generally expected in specific situations. American men, for example, shake hands with each other when first introduced. Japanese men bow.

It would be quite impossible here to catalog all the customs foreigners might find in the United States. It would be impossible, first, because there are so many situations in which customs influence or direct people's behavior. Some examples: what you say during introductions; whether you give a tip to someone who has served you; which rooms you may enter when you visit a stranger's home; whether you relinquish your bus seat to an older person; what help you can legitimately seek from your neighbor; when you give gifts, and what gifts are appropriate; what you do if you are a student and you arrive at a classroom after the class has started; and what you do if you are a businessman and your customer offers you an alcoholic drink your religion forbids you to take.

Another reason it would be impossible to list all American customs here is that there is so much variation in those customs. Even among the white, middle class whose norms are serving as the basis for our discussion of American culture, there is marked variation in customs. These variations are mainly along geographic lines. There are urban-rural differences, North-South differences, and coast-inland differences. Americans who relocate from a southern city to a western town or a New England village, for example, encounter countless customs that differ from the ones they have been familiar with.

Religious backgrounds also account for many differences in customs, not just those concerning religious practices but those concerning family life and holiday activities as well. Ethnic identities also produce differences in customs.

Although it is not possible to provide a catalog of American customs, it is possible to say a few useful things about them. We will try to do so here; in subsequent chapters there are many more references to specific American customs.

Just as foreigners expect to encounter different customs when they go abroad, the natives generally expect foreigners to be unfamiliar with local ways. In general, Americans will forgive foreigners who do not follow their customs if they believe the foreigners are generally polite and are not deliberately giving offense.

Many Americans, by the way, would not apply the word "customs" to their own routine and expected behaviors. Many

Americans are so convinced that their daily behavior is "natural" that they suppose only people from other countries have customs. Customs, in this view, are arbitrary restraints on the behavior people would engage in if they were free to act naturally—that is, the way Americans act.

Some Americans might acknowledge that they have customary behaviors surrounding certain holidays. Staying up until midnight on New Year's Eve is one such custom; having a meal of turkey, dressing, cranberry sauce, and pumpkin pie on Thanksgiving is another.

Of course, Americans (like everyone else) have thousands of other behaviors that can be called customary, a few examples of which appeared above. Most customary behaviors follow from the values and assumptions we have already talked about. Americans value independence and self-reliance, for example, so it is customary for them to encourage their children to express their opinions. They assume all people are more or less equal, so it is customary for them to talk in relatively informal ways with nearly everyone.

Other kinds of customary behaviors are more arbitrary. That is, they have no clear relationship to the basic values and world view that underlie the culture. Table manners are an example. Americans are taught to hold the fork in the left hand and the knife in the right while using the knife to cut their food, then to lay the knife aside and switch the fork to the right hand to eat. Europeans, by contrast, are taught to keep the knife in the right hand and the fork in the left at all times. This difference is arbitrary, unrelated to larger issues about individuality vs. interdependence, equality vs. hierarchical rankings, and so on.

Foreigners cannot be expected to learn all the customs that prevail in America. What they should try to learn is the relatively small number of behaviors that are considered unacceptable by most people in the United States or will nearly always evoke a quick, strong, negative reaction from Americans. What follows is not a complete listing of unacceptable behaviors— such a list would be impossible to devise—but a few guidelines intended to help foreign visitors avoid behaviors that are quite likely to get them into trouble with Americans.

Be punctual. Most Americans will feel offended if you are more than 10 to 15 minutes late for a meeting, appointment, or social engagement. If you must be late, try to give notice.

If you agree to meet someone, whether at the person's house or elsewhere, keep the appointment. It is particularly rude to accept an invitation to a person's home for a meal and then not appear.

Treat females with the same respect you accord males.

Treat clerks, waiters, secretaries, taxi drivers and other such people courteously.

When you are standing and talking to an American, stay at least an arm's length away unless (1) you are going to hit the person, (2) you are going to hug, caress, or kiss the person, or (3) the person has clearly indicated to you that he or she wants you closer. You can stand a bit closer than arm's length if you are side-to-side rather than face-to-face. Males will want to be particularly cautious about touching other males—except when shaking hands—unless they want to convey the impression that they feel a homosexual attraction to them. (This warning may seem overstated. No doubt foreign males will find American men who do not react adversely to other men who get close to them or touch them. But so many American men respond negatively to other men who get too close that foreign males are well advised to keep their distance, getting closer—if they want to—only after it is clear that doing so would be acceptable.)

Avoid bowing and other behavior that is intended to display deep respect for the other person. Most Americans become extremely uncomfortable if they are the object of such displays.

Beyond these points and those that emerge from the remaining pages of this book, readers will need other sources for learning about American customs. The best source, of course, is individual Americans. Just ask them what behavior is expected in particular situations. Explain, if you want to, that you are new to the place and are not familiar with the way certain things are done. Most Americans will be happy to try to answer your questions. If you encounter one who is not, try a different one.

PART II

★ ★ ★

Specific Aspects of American Life

In Part I we looked at some general characteristics of Americans. Here in Part II we will consider in more detail the way Americans generally think and behave in certain important areas of life. We will start with politics, not because Americans generally give prominence to that aspect of life, but because many foreign visitors do.

Other topics in Part II are family life; education; religion; the media; social relationships; male-female relationships; sports and recreation; shopping; driving; personal hygiene; getting things done in organizations; behavior in public places; studying (as done by students); business; and finally nonverbal communication, a topic that relates to most of the preceding ones.

Once again it is important to remember that what appears here are generalizations. There are exceptions to all of them. What Part II tries to capture are some distinctive features of American life that foreign visitors generally notice. Taking note of the ideas in Part II will help foreign visitors be prepared for and better understand aspects of American life that might otherwise seem incomprehensible.

CHAPTER 5

☆ ☆ ☆

Politics

Americans are quite proud of their political system. Whether they are well informed about politics (most are not) or whether they participate actively in political matters (many do not), they believe their political system has advantages most other political systems lack. They believe it protects their individual freedom, which is a value of supreme importance to them. They believe their system is, or can be, responsive to their wishes in ways other systems cannot be.

Paradoxically, most Americans have a rather negative view of politics and politicians. The system might be very good, but the people who operate within it might not be. As a group, politicians are generally seen as relatively unintelligent, excessively talkative, and somewhat devious. Government employees, too, are suspect. Many Americans suppose that the government has too many workers, and only a few who are diligent and productive enough to deserve the pay they get. Paradoxically, again, Americans generally expect and receive competent service from government employees.

Perhaps because they fear that a government can become "too strong" and thereby endanger citizens' freedom, Americans tolerate a political system that seems utterly inefficient to many people from other countries. The American system was, indeed, originally established in such a way as to prevent it from taking quick, concerted action in any but the most extreme circumstances. There is a "division of power," with various governmental responsibilities divided among the national, state, and local levels and, there is the "separation of powers" among the executive, legislative, and judicial branches—at both the national and state levels. There is the "two-party system," with two large and ideologically ambiguous parties competing for positions in the government.

This structure results in extreme decentralization that people from many other countries have difficulty understanding. The decentralization is most evident in the domestic realm, and somewhat less so in the conduct of foreign affairs. In both realms, though, the United States government has more internal impediments to action than most other governments do. American citizens tend to see that as an advantage, or at least as a price worth paying for the limits it puts on the government's ability to infringe on individual citizens' lives.

The administrative side of the government does not have the built-in "checks and balances" that keep the political side from acting decisively. Some administrative agencies are quite efficient. Others are less so. Among the least efficient, most observers would agree, is the Immigration and Naturalization Service, the one agency with which foreign visitors inevitably have dealings.

Americans feel very free to criticize their political leaders. The president, senators and congressmen, governors, mayors, and others are subject to public criticism so harsh that foreign visitors are sometimes shocked and embarrassed to see or hear it—even if they agree with it. But while they themselves feel free to criticize, Americans usually do not welcome criticisms that come from foreign visitors. "If you don't like it here, go back where you came from," is the reaction foreigners sometimes get when they make negative comments about American politics (as well as other aspects of American life).

Besides their pride in their system of government and their propensity to criticize their leaders, Americans have three other general ideas about politics that foreigners will want to understand: they believe firmly in what they call the "rule of law," they idealize compromise, and they conceive of politics as something separable from other aspects of life.

THE RULE OF LAW

The idea behind the "rule of law" is that impartial laws, not human beings with their irrational and arbitrary tastes and judgments, should govern the formal aspects of social interaction. "We live under a rule of law, not of men," American teachers tell their students. The students accept the idea. They believe that "no man is above the law," that laws apply equally to all people regardless of their wealth, personal connections, or station in life. Their faith in the rule of law explains the conviction many Americans held, and many foreigners could not understand, that President Richard Nixon should be removed from office as a result of his behavior in connection with what was called the "Watergate scandal." Nixon had broken the law and therefore should be punished, Americans believed, even if he was the president.

The belief in the rule of law goes beyond the realm of politics to other areas of life that are governed by formal rules and procedures. Getting a job with a government agency, for example, or getting a government grant for a research project, entails following published procedures and demonstrating that one meets the published requirements. Personal connections are not supposed to matter under the rule of law.

This is not to say that personal contacts, wealth, and social influence do not matter where laws and rules are concerned. They may. What is said above describes the ideal to which Americans subscribe. In reality, connections can sometimes help a person get a government job. Rich people can sometimes go unpunished for illegal behavior that poor people would be likely to be punished for. But in general the rule of law prevails, and Americans are proud that it does.

THE IDEAL OF COMPROMISE

A compromise is a settlement of differences in which both (or all) parties make some concessions to the other side. Both sides "give in" somewhat for the sake of reaching agreement. Americans are taught that compromise is a good thing. Mature people, in the general American view, resolve their differences through discussion and compromise. There are of course different ideas about what constitutes an acceptable level of compromise, but in general a political agreement that results from a compromise among contending parties is, by definition, a good thing.

Others may not share the American assumption that it is good to compromise. Compromise may be seen as abandoning one's principles, one's correct viewpoint. People who see compromise in that light are likely to take a negative view of those aspects of the American system that Americans themselves think are so positive.

POLITICS APART

Americans, perhaps more than people in any other country, believe that politics can be separated from other aspects of life. "Let's keep politics out of this," they will say, making the assumption that matters of official power do not enter into economic dealings, family structure, the efficiency of government services, and other aspects of life that do not involve the direct participation of politicians and government bodies. They will relate to other people without regard to their political opinions. They would generally rather not "talk politics." This approach seems quite naive to most Latins, Europeans, Arabs, and Africans, who tend to suppose that "politics is everything, and everything is politics."

Given their conception of politics as separate from other aspects of life, and their image of politicians as less than worthy people, it is not surprising that the portion of American citizens who actively participate in politics is rather small. Many American citizens have not gone through the simple procedure of registering to vote. Once they have registered they have the right to vote in national, state, and local elections, but Americans participate in elections at a lower rate than citizens of any other democratic country.

Beyond voting, other means of participating in politics are open to Americans. Those who have relatively strong opinions or convictions on political matters may volunteer to work in a candidate's election campaign or work on behalf of one or another political party. They may join organizations that seek to mobilize support on one side or the other of any controversial question. They may even run for elective office themselves.

Americans who do not want to get involved in politics but who need some information or decision from a government body are likely to turn to their elected representatives for help. Senators and congressmen maintain staffs whose job it is to respond to "constituents" who have asked for assistance of some kind. Americans believe it is their right to get such aid from the politicians who have been elected to represent them.

In sum, Americans tend to embody what to many is a curious combination of admiration for their political system in general and disdain for its particular operations. They criticize their leaders, but do not want foreigners to do so. They strongly believe in the value of the rule of law and of compromise. They think about politics as a separable aspect of life, one they can choose to ignore. Their low level of participation in politics, not to mention their general lack of interest in political affairs, seems inexplicable if not irresponsible to many visitors from abroad.

CHAPTER 6

☆ ☆ ☆

Family Life

When Americans use the term "family," they are usually refer-ring to a father, a mother, and their children. This is the so-called "nuclear family." Grandparents, aunts, uncles, cousins, and others who might be labeled "family" in many other coun-tries are "relatives" in American terminology. These usages reflect the fact that, for most Americans, the family is a small group of people, not an extended network.

Like many other aspects of American life, families are changing. Many observers attribute the principal changes evi-dent in American families in the mid-1980s to the feminist movement. Others say the difficult economic times are respon-sible. Whatever the reasons (remember this book is not about "why"), the traditional father-dominated family is becoming less common. There are more and more households in which both parents work, and in which the males have taken on household responsibilities that used to be left to females. There are more single-parent families (that is, households containing only one parent—usually the woman—and one or more chil-dren). Larger numbers of teenage children are employed, and thus have a disposable income of their own. It is increasingly common to find unmarried couples living together, unmarried women having children, and "blended families" that are com-posed of a man, a woman, and both of their children from previous marriages.

Until very recently the divorce rate in the United States increased slowly and steadily for many decades. There are signs that the rate may have diminished slightly in 1986.

48

Statistically, the "average family" (in 1985) had just 3.23 members. The average age at which people first marry has been increasing steadily since 1960. For males the average age at first marriage reached 25.5 in 1985, while for females it was 23.3. But the "average family" is hard to find in the real world. Generalizations one can make about the American family are few. Among those that seem safe are these:

However modern or liberated (from tradition) a family may be, there is likely to be at least some reflection of the traditional male-female role division. Traditionally, the female was responsible for matters inside the house: cleaning, caring for the children, shopping for groceries and clothing, and preparing meals. The male was responsible for things outside the house: maintaining the family car (or cars) and the yard. The man would be expected to take care of whatever home repairs and improvements were within his capabilities.

The children are expected to contribute at least in some measure to home maintenance. They are responsible for certain "chores," such as washing dishes, vacuuming carpets, and keeping their rooms clean. Children of different sexes may have responsibilities that reflect the traditional household responsibilities of their sex. Thus, boys are more likely to be responsible for mowing the lawn (under the father's supervision) and girls for washing dishes or elementary cooking (with the mother's guidance).

The children are not as heavily involved in schoolwork as children in many other countries are. American public schools tend to be less demanding than those in many other countries, and there are no standardized school-leaving examinations to give focus to children's academic efforts. Academic achievement gets less emphasis from the average American family than it does from families in many other places.

The children get considerable attention. Many American homes are what sociologists call "child-centered." That is, the children's perceived needs, interests, and preferences strongly influence the way in which the parents spend their time and money. Parents play with their young children. They send them to "preschool" and enroll them in lessons and classes of many kinds (music, dance, sports, arts). They arrange for their children to get together with other children their own age. They buy things their children want. They talk to their children as though the children were simply small adults, asking their opinions and, in some measure, taking those opinions into account when making decisions that affect the entire family. These child-centered families seem very busy, since each child has a schedule of lessons, practices, and social engagements.

The degree to which families are "child-centered" varies. From the viewpoint of most foreigners, though, American families are generally more child-centered than families in their own countries.

There is also variation in the degree to which American families are male-dominated. In some, the male holds the traditional dominant role. In others, the female and perhaps also the children have an active role in family decision-making.

Foreign visitors are often surprised to see how many American teenagers have jobs. The teenagers earn their own money for entertainment, clothes, or a car by delivering newspapers, cooking or washing dishes in a fast-food restaurant, mowing lawns, or other menial activity. Some save at least part of their income for college expenses. From the parents' viewpoint, having a job gives their children valuable training in acting independently, managing their time and money, and accepting responsibility for their own decisions. Having to get up early on a cold Sunday morning to deliver newspapers is conceived of as "good training" for a 13-year-old.

This discussion of American family life illustrates the manner in which some of the values and assumptions described in Chapter One are manifested in the family. Notions about independence, individuality, equality, and informality are all embodied in what takes place in families. Another notion that underlies American family dynamics is that of the "rebellious teenager." Americans assume that adolescence is inherently a period of turmoil. Teenagers are expected to be self-centered, moody, and uncooperative while they seek to "find themselves" or "establish their personal identities" as individuals separate from others in the family.

American parents generally expect that their children's lives will be at least as comfortable materially as their own, if not more so. When they think about their children's futures, they think about them mainly in terms of the jobs their children will get and how much income those jobs will produce. Once again, then, the basic values and assumptions underlying the culture—in this case the importance placed on achievement, work, and acquiring material goods—are taught and reinforced through the family.

In the stereotypic "average family," the children are ready to move out of the parents' house by the age of 18—that is, when they have completed secondary school. They may "go to college" (Americans use the term "college" to refer to any post-secondary educational institution) or they may seek a job. They might stay with the parents for another year or two, but after that they are expected to be "on their own."

Americans use the term "empty nest syndrome" to refer to the psychological impact on the parents, particularly the mother, of the last child's departure from home. If the parents have long devoted major attention to their children and the children eventually leave, the parents confront a sort of vacuum in their lives. What are they supposed to do with their extra time and energy? The "empty nest syndrome" is a combination of boredom, depression, and feeling of purposelessness that afflicts parents who no longer have their children around them on a daily basis. As an antidote, many women, after their children leave, are entering or re-entering the work-force or pursuing some social or political interest.

Sometimes the empty nest fills up again, at least temporarily. A child who has gone away to college may come home for the summers. A child who has gotten a job may lose it and be left without income to support a separate household. A child who got married may encounter marital difficulties or even get a divorce and return, sometimes with the grandchildren, to live in the parents' house.

Another major turning point in family life is likely to come when the parents' parents become enfeebled or die. Mr. Wilson's mother lived in a nursing home, a situation that is not unusual. Many aged parents live alone for as long as they possibly can before moving to a nursing home or taking up residence with one of their children. It is usually considered a difficult or awkward situation when an aged parent is living with grown children. Ideals about independence and self-sufficiency are so deeply imbued in most Americans that a situation of enforced dependency can be extremely uncomfortable for the elderly, infirm parent as well as for the children.

CHAPTER 7

☆ ☆ ☆

Education

"Anybody can get into college in the USA," it was common to hear Malaysians say. They were referring to the fact that at least some American post-secondary educational institutions have rather low admissions standards. Applicants who had no possibility of entering a Malaysian university could get into one in the States. Malaysians who remarked on the easy accessibility of American colleges and universities were comparing the American system unfavorably to that of the British, who once ruled Malaysia and who provided the model for Malaysia's educational system. Under the British approach, difficult school-leaving examinations are used to limit the number of people given places in post-secondary schools and to assure that the people who got those places were well qualified to be students.

On the other hand, these Malaysians would observe, "You [Americans] put men on the moon. So there must be something right about your system."

Many people interested in education get trapped into trying to answer the question, "Which is the better educational system, the American, the British, or some other?" That question cannot be answered. A more appropriate question is, "What are the advantages and disadvantages of the American educational system?" We will return to that question at the end of this chapter, after considering a number of issues related to it.

This chapter does not describe the structure of the U.S. system. Many other publications do a comprehensive job of explaining about elementary school, junior high and high school, community colleges, four-year colleges, universities, various academic degrees, and so on. One place to read about these matters is Clifford Sjogren's *Diversity, Accessibility, and Quality: A Brief Introduction to American Education for Non-Americans*, published in 1986 by the College Board.

After an overview of the ideals that guide the American system of education, this chapter discusses some of the social forces that are at work on American educational institutions and some contemporary issues facing schools in the United States. All this will help foreign visitors understand what they hear about schools in this country and will lead into the comments about the system's advantages and disadvantages.

GUIDING IDEALS

Access to education

The American educational system is based on the idea that as many people as possible should have access to as much education as possible. This fact alone distinguishes the U.S. system from most others, since in most others the objective is as much to screen people out as it is to keep them in. The U.S. system has no standardized examinations whose results systematically prevent students from going on to higher levels of study, as the British and many other systems do. Through secondary school and sometimes in post-secondary institutions as well, the American system tries to accommodate students even if their academic aspirations and aptitudes are not high, even if they are physically (and in some cases mentally) handicapped, and even if their native language is not English.

The idea that as many people as possible should have as much education as possible is, of course, an outcome of the Americans' assumptions (discussed in Chapter One) about equality among people. These assumptions do not mean that everyone has an equal opportunity to enter Harvard, Stanford, or other highly competitive post-secondary institutions. Admission to such institutions is generally restricted to the most academically able. The less able can usually matriculate in a post-secondary institution, as the Malaysians observed, but one of lower quality.

As of March, 1982, only 3 per cent of all Americans aged 25 or more had completed less than five years of elementary school. Seventy-one per cent of those 25 or more had completed four years of high school or gone beyond that, and 17.7 per cent had completed four or more years of post-secondary education. The median number of school years completed was 12.6. The number of tertiary (that is, post-secondary) students per 100,000 inhabitants was 5355. Some contrasts: The number of tertiary students per 100,000 in the population was 4006 in Canada. In no other country, according to UNESCO data, was the number of post-secondary students above 2700 per 100,000. Korea had 2696 tertiary students per 100,000 inhabitants; Japan, 2030; the USSR 1970; Argentina, 1890; Hong Kong, 1353; Malaysia, 472; and Ethiopia, 48.

Naturally, an educational system that retains as many people as the American system does is likely to enroll a broader range of students than a system that seeks to educate only the few who seem especially suited for academic work. In the American system, academic rigor tends to come later than it does in most other systems. In many instances, American students do not face truly demanding educational requirements until they seek a graduate (that is, post-baccalaureate) degree. Many other systems place heavy demands on students as early as their primary years—though college may be far less demanding, as is the case in Japan.

Universal literacy

A second ideal underlying the United States educational system is that of producing a society that is 100 per cent literate. All American states (in the U.S., education is governed by state and local bodies, not by the national government, as we shall see below) have compulsory attendance laws that require young people to attend school until a specified age (16 in most states, 14 or 15 in a very few, and 17 or 18 in about 10). The goal of 100 per cent literacy has yet to be achieved, and may never be achieved, but it remains the stated goal.

Equal opportunity

A third ideal, again in keeping with the Americans' assumptions about equality, is that of providing comparable educational programs to everyone, regardless of race, handicap, or social standing. This is another ideal that has yet to be achieved.

Local control

Fourth, the American educational system is based on the ideal of local control. There is no national ministry of education. (There is a United States Department of Education, but it has no power over individual schools.) State departments of education have some influence over the curriculum of primary and secondary schools, whether they are public (that is, supported by taxes) or private (that is, supported by tuition and other non-governmental sources). It is local bodies, though, that bear the main responsibility for guiding educational institutions. Public primary and secondary schools are under the general direction of bodies that are usually called boards of education or school boards. Those boards hire and fire superintendents and sometimes principals, oversee the curriculum of the schools in their jurisdiction, and review teacher performance. There is a separate board of education, usually elected by the public, for each "school district." A school district may be no larger than one city or county; each state has many, many school districts.

Decentralization is evident at the post-secondary level too. Most colleges and universities, whether they are public or private, have their own "board of regents" or some such body to provide general guidance over an institution's policies. Sometimes all the public colleges and universities in a given state will be guided by a single board. The more specific policies that govern colleges and universities are made not by these boards but by faculty and administrators at each separate institution. Faculty groups set curriculum and graduation requirements; individual professors decide what they will include in their courses and how they will evaluate their students.

At all levels of education, standards are set and maintained by regional accrediting associations to which the schools subscribe, not by the government.

Few if any countries have educational systems as thoroughly decentralized as that in the United States. Many foreign visitors have difficulty comprehending the fact that so much control over educational matters rests at the local level, and that there is no federal body empowered to override local decisions.

Parental involvement

Fifth, many primary and secondary schools idealize "parental involvement" in children's education. The schools, through meetings and printed information sent to parents, encourage the parents to become acquainted with their children's teachers, to talk to their children about what happens in school, and to confer and work together with the teachers should a child encounter any difficulty that interferes with academic progress or social adjustment. This call for parental involvement may seem odd to parents from countries where education is considered the teachers' business, not one in which parents have a special role.

Analysis and synthesis

A sixth ideal has to do with the assumptions Americans make about the basic nature of knowledge and learning. The assumption is that only a certain part of all that is potentially knowable is already known. Scholars and students—mainly advanced scholars and graduate students—work at the "frontiers of knowledge" to discover new information or conceive of new ways to understand or interpret what is already known. Learning at all levels is thus considered not just a process of

memorizing as much as one can of a more or less fixed body of
knowledge that already exists in books and in scholars' minds.
Learning is an enterprise of exploration, experimentation, analysis, and synthesis. Students can engage in those activities, in
the American view, just as well as teachers and professors can.
The ideal educational situation is therefore one in which students are learning the skills of analysis and synthesis and are
applying those skills to the process of "discovering new knowledge." Students who come to the United States from educational systems that rely on memorization and reverent acceptance
of teachers' words have academic difficulty until they learn the
intellectual attitudes and skills that go along with analyzing
and synthesizing the material they study.

Well-rounded people

Finally, the American educational system seeks to turn
out "well-rounded people." Such people might have specialized
knowledge in some area, but they are all expected to have a
general acquaintance with many disciplines. Having passed
through a system that requires them to study some mathemat-
ics, some English, some humanities, some science, and some
social science (and perhaps a foreign language), they presumably have an array of interests and can understand information
from many fields of study. Thus, specialization in the American system comes later than it does in many other systems.
Students are required to take courses that they themselves
might not be interested in and that might not have any apparent relationship to their career aspirations.

Although not an "ideal," there is a final sentiment that
must be taken into account as one tries to understand the
American educational system. That sentiment is anti-intellec-
tualism. As Chapter Three sought to make clear, most Americans are suspicious of theorizing and "intellectualizing." They
want to see practical results from time and money spent. Sec-
ondary-school and university graduates are expected to be well-
rounded to an extent, but not to the extent that they cannot do
anything "useful." Americans are unimpressed by most learn-

ing that is done just for the sake of learning. They have no general reverence for university teachers who live in an "ivory tower" that is divorced from the real world.

SOCIAL FORCES AFFECTING AMERICAN EDUCATION

A few aspects of the social context in which American education operates are worth mentioning. The first has to do with the social status or degree of respect ascribed to people who are involved in education.

American teachers (that term usually applies to people who teach in kindergarten through grade 12, the final grade in secondary school) do not enjoy high status in the society. Respondents to a 1985 Gallup Poll placed teachers well below physicians, clergymen, and bankers in terms of their prestige or status in the community. Judges, lawyers, and public school principals were also rated above teachers. Funeral directors and local political officeholders were seen as having nearly as much prestige or status as teachers did. Teachers are not well paid. Their working conditions are usually less comfortable than those of workers in many other areas. They are not as well respected as are people who actually "do" something rather than "just" teach.

Nor are college and university professors generally held in the high regard they are in many other countries. There are some exceptions—mainly those who have made particularly noteworthy contributions to science (not the humanities, usually, because the humanities are not "practical")—but professors are often viewed as people who are teaching because they are not capable of doing anything else.

In some societies students are generally respected, since being a student is relatively unusual and requires special effort. Not so in the United States. Nearly everyone under the age of 18 is a student, and so are many who are older. Under these circumstances, students are rarely accorded special respect.

Finally there is the matter of teacher education. In most colleges and universities, people who teach prospective teachers are at or near the bottom of the status hierarchy. "Educationists" are looked down upon by most others within academia.

Another aspect of the society that affects education is the amount of money devoted to its support. Education competes with other public enterprises that need money. Some states consistently put a higher percentage of their budgets into education than others, but none consistently gives education its highest priority. Most educators believe their institutions are always under-funded.

The third social factor influencing education is politics. In some states and communities, contemporary political conflicts are directly reflected in the administration of educational institutions. School boards may get into debates about the role of such things as "peace education," "sex education," "drug education," or "non-sexist, non-racist education" in elementary schools. State governors may appoint their political supporters to positions on the board of regents that governs the state's major public university.

However, the degree to which political conflicts are manifested in educational institutions in America is probably minimal. National political conflicts, as opposed to local ones, rarely have a direct influence on the staffing, governance, or policies of American educational institutions. Except during times of national crisis (for example, the war in Vietnam), American students are generally non-political, though small, vocal groups of students periodically engage in attention-getting activities in support of their views on major social and political questions, such as disarmament, women's rights, and nuclear power.

ISSUES FACING AMERICAN SCHOOLS

Like all other social institutions, educational institutions are the subject of continuing controversy about one issue or another. Some of these issues confront just primary or secondary schools; some confront just post-secondary institutions. Some touch institutions at all levels.

An issue facing schools at all levels has to do with financial support. There are always people who believe schools should get more public money than they do, and others who think they are already getting enough, if not too much. In times of economic slowdown debates about the quantity of money that should go to schools are almost constant.

Assessing the quality of educational institutions is another persistent issue. How does one determine whether individual teachers and schools in general are doing a good job? This question cannot be answered in precise, quantifiable terms. So it continues to vex educational administrators, politicians, and the public.

At the primary and secondary level, there is frequently controversy about the quality of textbooks. Have they been made too simple? Have controversial issues been avoided so that potential textbook buyers are less likely to be offended by a book's contents? Have "facts" been distorted to make them more palatable to potential consumers?

Some other recurrent controversial issues are these:

whether primary and secondary schools should require, encourage, or allow students to pray to a supreme being during the school day. (See the discussion about "separation of church and state" in the next chapter.);

whether particular books (usually they are famous novels) that contain profane or sex-related language should be assigned in classes or available in secondary school libraries;

whether religious symbols should be used in school activities related to national holidays, especially Christmas, that have religious origins;

what students should be taught about the origin of mankind, specifically, whether they should be taught the theory that mankind evolved from lower animals or the theory that mankind was created by a supreme being;

what measures can appropriately be taken to bring about racial integration or racial balance in public schools. (Particular controversy has surrounded the practice of "busing" children to schools away from their own neighborhoods in order to achieve racially-balanced enrollments.);

what is the proper balance between general or "liberal" education and education or training intended to prepare students to work in particular fields;

whether female secondary school students should be allowed to participate on athletic teams that are traditionally all-male.

Schools are blamed, at least by some people, for many of the problems or failures of society in general. Schools are called upon to add one concern or another to their curriculum in order to remedy perceived social problems. Thus, schools are called upon to give more attention to such matters as values and ethics; racial integration; preserving the environment; world peace; sex education; the special needs of minority students, non-English-speaking students, physically and mentally handicapped students, intellectually gifted students, and female students; health and hygiene; and international education. In most other countries issues such as these would not be placed in the domain of schools, but in that of the family, churches, political parties, or some other social institution.

The fact that the American educational system is so decentralized makes it possible for these issues to come up again and again in place after place. Different solutions evolve in different localities. There is no uniform, authoritative answer to them, as there might be in a country with a centralized educational system.

ADVANTAGES AND DISADVANTAGES

From what has been said above, many of the American educational system's advantages and disadvantages become clear.

The system provides formal education for a relatively large portion of the population, but the quality of that education is not as high as it might be if the system were more selective. (Most experts agree that people who earn Ph.D. degrees in the United States are as well prepared to work in their disciplines as are people who earn Ph.D.'s in other systems. Below the

Ph.D. level, though, many systems offer more depth in students' chosen disciplines than the American one does.)

The system's decentralization serves to insulate educational institutions from national political entanglements and give citizens some voice in what happens in their local schools. Schools can modify their curricula to accommodate needs and conditions that pertain only to their own areas. On the other hand, the decentralization makes it relatively easy for an outspoken and committed minority in a given community to embroil local schools in controversy. The decentralization also makes it possible for particular schools to maintain low standards if they wish or feel compelled to do so.

"Well-rounded" people, such as those the American system hopes to produce, stand a better chance of becoming "good citizens" (as the Americans use that term) since they have a general familiarity with many topics and can keep themselves informed about matters of public policy. On the other hand, well-rounded people might not be as well equipped to begin working in specific occupations because they have not learned as much in school about specific areas of endeavor as have students whose systems permitted earlier and more intensive specialization.

The American educational system, like any other, is integrally related to the values and assumptions of the society that surrounds it. American ideas about equality, individualism, and freedom underlie the educational system. Whatever its advantages and disadvantages, the system will retain its current general characteristics as long as the values and assumptions that predominate in the surrounding society continue to hold sway.

CHAPTER 8

☆ ☆ ☆

Religion

"In my country," said a Syrian physician who was studying in the United States, "religion is a part of everyday life, like it is in other Middle Eastern countries. Even if a person is not particularly religious, Islam will still affect that person's life because it is an important part of our culture. Religion is not just praying like it is here in America."

Americans do indeed tend to separate religion from other parts of their personal lives in a way that many foreigners have difficulty understanding. We will return to the topic of religion in Americans' daily lives after considering some general information about religion in the United States. This chapter also specifies some exceptions to our generalizations about Americans and religion, and it offers some suggestions for foreign visitors who want to learn more about religion in the States or to practice their own religion while here.

THE GENERAL CONTEXT

Americans learn in their history classes that many of the Europeans who originally settled here were escaping "religious persecution" in their own countries. They were adherents of religions that were out of favor with their governments, and they wanted to find a place where they could practice their religions without governmental interference. What evolved from this concern, when the government of the United States became established, was the doctrine of "separation of church and state." What that doctrine means is that the government is not to give official support to any particular religion, nor is it to prevent individuals from practicing the religion of their choice.

Although the doctrine of separation of church and state is one of the foundation stones of the American system of government, it has not resolved all the issues relative to the relationship between religion and government. Far from it. There are varying interpretations of what constitutes a "religion" and varying ideas about what constitutes governmental support for or opposition to a religion. Many fundamentalist Christians disapprove of the church-state separation doctrine and believe the government should actively support their own views and oppose those of others.

Therefore, there are recurrent public debates and controversies about aspects of the separation between church and state. Controversial issues that have arisen in the recent past include these:

Can the government properly help buy textbooks for church-related primary and secondary schools?

Should public universities allow the distribution of free Bibles to students on their campuses?

Should movies that are less than reverential in their treatment of the Christian deity be permitted to be shown?

Can municipal governments properly mount Christian-related displays on public property at Christmas time?

For a vocal minority of Americans, issues such as these are extremely important. Whether they are on one side of the debate or the other, they see these church-state issues as closely related to their country's ultimate destiny. Some believe their country's basic ideals are threatened by violations of the doctrine of separation of church and state. Others believe their country is threatened by a severe decline in adherence to Christian values.

Although there are these disagreements about the details of the church-state separation, Americans generally take pride in the religious freedom their governmental system provides. While the most prevalent religiously-related values are Judeo-Christian ones brought to the country by its early European settlers, the fact is that many different religions are now practiced in the United States. The principal ones are Catholicism, Protestantism (which has numerous denominations), and Judaism. According to the 1986 *Yearbook of American and Canadian Churches*, 142,172,138 Americans, or 59.5 per cent of the population, belonged to some religious group. The largest groups were Catholics, Baptists (with 15 different subdivisions), Methodists (10 subdivisions), and Lutherans, who recently merged a number of their larger subdivisions. About 2,000,000 Moslems live in the United States. Some of the many smaller religious groups, with membership numbering no more than a few thousand each, are the Anglican Orthodox, Baha'i, Buddhist Churches of America, Albanian Orthodox Diocese of America, the Coptic Orthodox Church, and the Vedanta Society.

Clearly the large majority of those practicing a religion in America are Christians. And, although the government does not officially lend its power and authority to the Christian viewpoint, the fact is that Christian traditions and holidays enjoy special standing in the society. Non-Christians sometimes complain that their traditions and viewpoints get inadequate recognition and respect.

Many Americans are not affiliated with any religion and do not attend any church. Such people may be atheists, that is, people who have decided they do not believe any supreme being exists. They may be people who consider themselves Christians but who do not subscribe to any of the denominations that comprise what is called "organized religion." Or they may be people who are not interested in religious matters and do not consider religion important to them.

Adherents of the various religions practiced in the United States are not distributed randomly in the population. There are groupings by geographic area, ethnic heritage, and social class. For example, Lutherans dominate in much of the state of Minnesota, where most early white settlers were from the Lutheran countries of Scandinavia. Eastern urban areas have concentrations of Catholics and Jews. The southern and southwestern parts of the United States are sometimes called the "Bible belt" in recognition of the fact that fundamentalist Protestants are especially prominent there, and the state of Utah is largely Mormon.

Americans of Irish, Italian, and Latin American descent are likely to be Catholics, if they subscribe to any religion. Most lower and lower-middle class black people who are affiliated with a church are Baptists. Episcopalians are usually from the wealthier stratum of the society, and highly educated people predominate among Unitarians.

Relationships among various religious groups in the United States are normally peaceful and are sometimes even quite harmonious.

A religious or quasi-religious phenomenon that has recently gained public notice in the United States is that of "cults." Cults are defined or described in various ways. In general they seek the total involvement and commitment of their members, who are expected to give up most of their material possessions and join with fellow believers in a life devoted to worship, contemplation, and the search for additional adherents. Some cults have a fundamentalist Christian outlook; others are based on Indian or Oriental religions or philosophies. Many Americans consider cults dangerous because they appear to rob members of their individuality and freedom of choice. Branches of cults may be found in large cities, on large university campuses, and in rural areas.

While it may be instructive for foreigners to know something about the doctrine of separation of church and state, the number and variety of religions practiced in the United States, the numbers of people who subscribe to each denomination, and the nature of the relationships among various religious groups, it is probably more helpful to understand the role religion plays in the daily lives of individual Americans. After all, it is individual Americans that foreigners encounter, not doctrines or religions or churches.

RELIGION AND INDIVIDUAL AMERICANS

To be religious in America means different things to different people. The general concept of the purpose of religion is that it provides spiritual guidance for people, helping them behave according to the tenets of brotherly love, forgiveness, charity, and humility. The most common understanding of "being religious" means belonging to a church and attending it regularly. ("Church" is used broadly here, to encompass not just Christian places of worship but also others, such as synagogues, temples, and meeting halls.) People are considered more religious than average if they more or less regularly participate in church-related activities on days other than the Sabbath (Saturday for Jews and Adventists and Sunday for most Christians). Religious families may say a prayer of thanks (called "grace") before eating each dinner they take in their homes. Religious people might, as the Syrian physician suggested, say prayers at times other than during Sabbath services.

However, many people who consider themselves Christians do not attend church regularly. They may attend as infrequently as once or twice a year, on Easter Sunday and Christmas Eve—two special days on the Christian calendar.

Whether or not they consider themselves religious, Americans are likely to turn to a religious official to perform the ceremonies associated with marriage and death.

Being religious, then, is generally defined more in terms of participating in formal church-related activities than it is in terms of adhering to a particular set of beliefs or behaviors. It is therefore possible for Americans to separate the religious aspect of their lives from other aspects. For many Americans, Sunday (or at least Sunday morning) is for religion.

As was suggested in Chapter Two, most Americans consider their religious beliefs and activities to be private matters. They do not readily discuss religion with other people whom they do not know well or who are not known to share their religious views. Americans will not usually ask each other, "What is your religion?" or, "Do you go to church?" Such questions are considered too personal. Discussion and debate about theological issues is not common.

EXCEPTIONS

There are important exceptions to some of what has been said so far. First, there are certain religious groups, mainly fundamentalist Christian, whose members consider it their duty to try to "convert" others to their own religions. Members of these groups will readily bring up the subject of religion and will try to induce people who do not belong to their group to become members. (It is not unusual for such people to single out foreigners, especially young unmarried ones, as likely candidates for conversion.)

Second, there are some communities—the Lutherans in Minnesota, Mormons in Utah, and Quakers in Pennsylvania are a few of many examples—where virtually everyone belongs to the same church. In those communities people's religious views are likely to be known by many people and talked about rather freely.

Third, even though the American constitution calls for separation of church and state, there are conspicuous examples of religious symbols and activities in public life. American coins bear the words, "In God we trust." The pledge of allegiance Americans say to their flag refers to the United States as a nation "under God." Each session of the United States Congress, Supreme Court, and some other official bodies opens with an invocation (that is, a prayer for divine guidance). Some people are concerned about the apparent contradiction between the church-state separation doctrine and these official uses of religious symbols and activities. Most people, though, accept them as harmless rituals.

Fourth, candidates for and holders of elective office at the national and sometimes the state level often make their religious views and activities quite public. They announce what church they belong to, and they have themselves photographed attending church, usually in the company of their families. All this is usually regarded as part of an effort to portray themselves as wholesome, right-minded people who deserve the public's trust.

SUGGESTIONS FOR FOREIGN VISITORS

If they are interested in Americans and religion, one of the things foreign visitors will want to do is attend church services to observe the rituals. Newspapers list the times church services begin, and most churches welcome people who simply stop in to observe or to join a service.

Students will find "campus ministries" on many U.S. campuses. Campus ministries are affiliated with particular churches (although they often cooperate with each other in carrying out large-scale activities). They sponsor meetings, activities, and services intended specifically for young adults. Campus ministries are often a recognized part of a campus community and may even have official roles in school activities such as orientation, counseling, and guidance.

Of course, attending services and seeing rituals is not enough to give a foreign visitor a comprehensive understanding of religion in the United States. Visitors will want to talk to individual Americans about their ideas concerning religion. That can be difficult, as has been said. But it can be done. Once they have established a reasonably secure relationship with an American, or are for whatever reason confident that it is safe to do so, foreign visitors can bring up the topic of religion with particular Americans and talk about it with them. Taking care not to generalize too much, they can then reach their own conclusions about what "religion" and "being religious" means to Americans.

CHAPTER 9

☆ ☆ ☆

The Media

In some ways it seems pointless to talk here about the American media. American television programs, motion pictures, records, and tapes are available in all but the most remote parts of the world. American actors, actresses, and singers are familiar figures almost everywhere. The American public's appetite for glamorous and exciting movies and TV shows seems to be widely shared.

But there are some points about the American media (referring mainly to television and motion pictures) that might help foreign visitors have a more accurate understanding of them. Three general topics will be discussed here: the question of what makes the American media "American," Americans' own views of their media, and misconceptions about America the media promote in other countries.

WHAT IS AMERICAN ABOUT THE AMERICAN MEDIA

There is no authoritative answer to the question of what makes the American media distinctively American. Different people will have different opinions on the matter. A few brief opinions are offered here.

Many movie and TV stories mirror the values and assumptions to which most Americans adhere. Among them: admiration for the individual who disregards other people's opinions and does what he wants to do; admiration for the individual who somehow outwits or bests the "establishment" or the "authorities;" a faith that good will triumph over evil; glorification of people who are young and physically attractive; glorification of people who earn large amounts of money or who have acquired impressive quantities of material goods; and a fixation on the action-filled life, as opposed to the contemplative one.

Characteristics of contemporary American life that many foreigners find objectionable are also conveyed—perhaps in an exaggerated form—through movies and television programs: a lack of intellectual depth; a larger concern for appearance than for substance; a fixation on sex, as manifested by the large-breasted women and hairy-chested men who populate many popular films and TV programs; an almost morbid interest in violence, as manifested by the large number and variety of ways in which television and motion picture performers do harm to other people; and a fascination with "gadgets," with new technological devices that enable people to do things with less effort.

The American media are driven by competition for money. In that sense they epitomize the American economic system. They are always looking for new ways to attract viewers and buyers. They experiment, trying new things and dropping old ones. Trends and fads in television programs and motion pictures come and go with striking rapidity. Stars are in heavy demand one day and are forgotten the next.

The media are leaders in the search for popular applications of new technologies. Satellite television is one example of the presumably beneficial outcomes of competition for audience attention and loyalty. Other examples are satellite transmission of material to be printed, better and less expensive video cameras, computer graphics on television, and modern public-opinion sampling techniques, such as those television and radio use to determine audience interests and responses.

AMERICANS' VIEWS OF THEIR MEDIA

In America, as elsewhere, consumers vote with their dollars. If a motion picture producer makes a science fiction movie featuring creatures that visit the earth from outer space and the movie attracts large audiences, then there will be more movies with a similar theme. If a newspaper sells larger numbers of copies when it begins carrying more articles about the sex lives of well-known television actresses, the newspaper will carry more such articles.

American consumers also vote by responding to surveys. Radio and television stations regularly "poll" audiences to find out what people are listening to or watching, and to find out what potential audiences want to see and hear. A program with a low "audience rating" soon goes off the air.

Thus, American audiences can be said to get what they want from their media. The fact that American movies and television programs and performers are so popular elsewhere suggests that what the American public wants does not differ dramatically from what audiences elsewhere want.

Some Americans (including some media executives) praise radio and television for providing huge amounts of free or inexpensive entertainment for the American people and for giving Americans common experiences that create bonds of understanding among them. Some also laud television for raising the aspirations of lower-class Americans. Seeing the material well-being middle- and upper-class Americans enjoy might induce members of the lower class to work harder and save more, so they can improve their own position. (Others argue that the poor see the affluence depicted on TV and become discouraged at ever bridging the gap.)

This is not to say that all Americans are satisfied with the quality of their television, radio, and newspapers. They are not. Professional media critics and other thoughtful people argue that there is a larger audience for quality programming than the media decision-makers, especially those in television, recognize or admit. They believe television and many newspapers "pander" to unsophisticated tastes and should try to elevate the intellectual level of their products.

On the other hand, there are those who argue that many high-quality programs do in fact appear on commercial television, even if they are difficult to find amidst the more trivial broadcasts.

Foreign visitors wanting assistance in identifying television programs that might interest them can refer to the television review pages of major newspapers (especially the Sunday editions) and magazines.

Some Americans criticize their media, especially television, for being racist (by showing only white people as responsible, important individuals), sexist (by portraying women as "sex objects" rather than as whole human beings), violent, and inadequately concerned with realizing their potential for educating the public. They criticize the media for providing only superficial treatment of complex topics and events and for distracting Americans from important issues. They applaud the non-commercial "public" radio and television networks for at least attempting to provide in-depth analysis of current issues and "serious" entertainment programs. They also recognize that some newspapers (for example, the *New York Times*, *Washington Post*, and *Christian Science Monitor*) and magazines provide substantive coverage and commentary on current affairs.

MISCONCEPTIONS THE MEDIA PROMOTE

A Middle Eastern graduate student at the University of Pittsburgh was very unhappy about his housing arrangement. He had come to Pittsburgh with the idea that he would live in an apartment such as one he had seen portrayed in a recently-popular American movie. In that movie the main male actor had taken a job as manager of a small apartment complex. The apartments were modest, clean, and attractive. There was a swimming pool on the grounds. Most of the tenants were airline stewardesses (such people are now called "flight attendants"), who frequently sat around the pool in skimpy bathing suits and who were free with their sexual favors.

The student did not find such a place to live in Pittsburgh. Nor would he have found one anywhere else in the States. The movie had misled him into some false conceptions about the people and life in this country. Modest, clean, and attractive apartments are indeed available (although not usually near universities), and many have swimming pools. But the addition of the readily-available flight attendants took the story into the land of fantasy.

The movie was not intended to mislead foreigners. Its purpose was to earn money, which means it had to attract audiences in America. American audiences are attracted by novelty, glamour (as they themselves define it), and action. Americans view their movies and television programs in the context of their own real-life experiences, so they have information on the basis of which to interpret them more or less accurately. Most Americans will know, for example, that apartment complexes like the one the graduate student sought exist "only in the movies."

People abroad who see American films and television programs and who read American publications do not have the same context for understanding what they see and read. They inevitably relate American media products to their own experiences in their own countries, and the result is often misunderstanding and misconception.

One of the main misconceptions TV and movies convey abroad is that American women are nearly all readily available for sexual activity. Other misconceptions films and TV convey (again, not deliberately) include these:

The United States is composed of New York City, Chicago, Disneyland, Las Vegas, Hollywood, San Francisco, and Texas (at least Dallas).

Most American women are beautiful (according to contemporary Western standards) and most American men are handsome (according to the same standards). Those who are not beautiful or handsome are criminals, deceitful people, and members of the lower class.

Violent crime is an ever-present threat in all parts of the country.

Average Americans are rich and usually do not have to work to get money.

Average Americans live in large, modern, shiny houses or apartments.

Most things in America are large, modern, and shiny.

There is a stratum of American society in which most people are non-white, physically ugly, uneducated, and dedicated to violence.

High-speed automobile chases are frequently seen on American streets.

Non-white people are inferior to white people.

Foreigners who come to the United States with open minds will see for themselves that these images are inaccurate. Foreign visitors are well advised to take stock of the ideas they have about America from TV shows and movies they have seen, and then to consider carefully how well those ideas fit with what they actually see and hear in this country.

CHAPTER 10

☆ ☆ ☆

Social Relationships

Writing about "Why I Love America," British-born journalist Henry Fairlie recounted this memory:

> One spring day, shortly after my arrival, I was walking down the long, broad street of a suburb, with its sweeping front lawns (all that space), its tall trees (all that sky), and its clumps of azaleas (all that color). The only other person on the street was a small boy on a tricycle. As I passed him, he said "Hi!"—just like that. No four-year-old boy had ever addressed me without an introduction before. Yet here was this one, with his cheerful "Hi!" Recovering from the culture shock, I tried to look down stonily at his flaxen head, but instead, involuntarily, I found myself saying in return: "Well—hi!" He pedaled off, apparently satisfied. He had begun my Americanization.

The word "Hi!", Fairlie goes on to say,

> is a democracy. (I come from a country where one can tell someone's class by how they say "Hallo!" or "Hello!" or "Hullo," or whether they sat it at all.) But [in America] anyone can say "Hi!" Anyone does. (*The New Republic*, July 4, 1983, p.12)

Like many foreigners, Fairlie was struck, even stunned, by the degree of informality and egalitarianism that prevails among Americans. Anyone can say "Hi!" to anyone. First names are used almost immediately. People (most of them) seem warm and friendly from the very start. Fairlie remembers his first meetings with the Suffragan Bishop of Washington and with President Lyndon B. Johnson. Both greeted him with, "Hi,

Henry!" In most countries, such a thing simply would not happen.

But there is a difference between friendliness and friendship. While most Americans seem relatively warm and approachable upon first encounter, they later come to seem to many foreign visitors to be remote and unreachable. "Superficial" is the word many longer-term foreign visitors use to describe Americans' relationships with other people. Some of them believe that it is only with foreigners that Americans tend to make friends slowly, if they make them at all. More astute visitors notice that Americans tend to be remote and unreachable even among themselves. They are "very private," keeping their personal thoughts and feelings to themselves. They are difficult to get to know.

Foreign visitors sometimes feel betrayed by Americans whom they meet and who seem so kind and interested at first, but who later fail to allow new acquaintances to know them as individuals. The initial "Hi!" comes to seem dishonest or misleading as the small talk continues, the feelings do not show, and ideas about important topics remain hidden. "They seem cold, not really human," one Brazilian woman said. "They just can't let themselves go."

It seems to be the case that many Americans are simply not available for the close "friendship" relationships that many foreigners have had (and taken for granted) at home and assume they will find in America. Many Americans are simply too busy to have the time that is required to get to know another person well. Many have moved their residence from one place to another in the past and assume they will do so again, and they prefer not to establish intimate friendships that will be painful to leave. Americans have been taught, as was discussed in Chapter One, to idealize independent, self-reliant individuals. Such individuals are likely to avoid becoming too dependent on other people or allowing others to become dependent on them. They remain apart from others. They do not know how to do otherwise.

Americans typically assume that when people gather to socialize, they must undertake some activity together. They may go bowling or to a movie, play cards, or "have a few drinks." Americans generally do not have the idea that it can be pleasant or rewarding to sit and talk with other people for extended periods. (Americans would probably say "just sit" and "just talk.") Their discomfort is often evident if they are forced to sit and interact with people they do not know fairly well.

Once again it is important to recall that there are exceptions to these generalizations. Some Americans are willing to devote the time that is necessary to get to know others well and to develop close friendships. They will talk openly with their friends about personal thoughts and feelings that other Americans rarely reveal.

So far we have been generalizing about Americans' behavior toward people they have just met and about their behavior with respect to friendship. The points made so far are the ones foreign visitors most commonly make when they talk about their experiences with Americans. The subject of social relationships is a complex one, and comments on some other aspects of social relationships in America are in order. What follows is information and ideas about meeting new people, relationships prescribed by roles, courtesy, schedules, gifts, and sex roles and friendship. The chapter closes with some suggestions for foreign visitors who want to meet and develop relationships with Americans.

MEETING NEW PEOPLE

Henry Fairlie, who was quoted at the beginning of the chapter, implied that in his native country one person does not usually talk to another until the two have been introduced. So it is in many countries, but it is not so in the United States. Of course, acquaintances often begin when people are introduced to each other, but they may begin when one person simply starts a conversation with another.

People meet each other in shops, classrooms, buses, offices, and, as Henry Fairlie learned, on the sidewalk. Anyone can say "Hi!" to anyone and can stop to ask a question. (Asking a question is a more common way of opening a spontaneous conversation than is making a statement.) A tone of friendly informality is nearly always appropriate. Those people who do not wish to be engaged in a conversation with someone to whom they have not been introduced will make that fact clear by their response.

Chapter Two discussed the "small talk" topics that are common among Americans. They are appropriate for interactions with new people. Foreigners meeting Americans will want to keep in mind the other aspects of communicative style that were discussed in Chapter Two—the favorite mode of interaction, the depth of involvement sought, and so on. Remember that Americans, like everyone else, prefer to employ their accustomed communicative style. In their country, their style prevails.

More ideas about initiating interactions with Americans appear in the final section of this chapter.

RELATIONSHIPS PRESCRIBED BY ROLES

The anthropologist Edward Hall (in a famous book called *The Silent Language*) has described the United States as a "low context culture," meaning that there are relatively few rules or guidelines to prescribe behavior in particular situations. In a "high context culture," such as those of the Middle East and much of Latin America, there tend to be agreed-upon guidelines for behavior in many specific situations. For example, a proper young Latin American woman does not allow herself to be in the company of a man unless some responsible third party is present. That is the "rule" and everyone knows it. In a high context culture there are such rules for many situations.

In the United States there are far fewer situations in which people's behavior is governed by widely agreed-upon rules. Still, there are some roles that generally entail certain expected behaviors. Such roles include those of customer, tenant, neighbor, and co-worker. There are regional and institutional variations in the behaviors described here, but a few generalizations can be offered:

Customer

When they are shopping, dining out, or otherwise using the services of clerks, waiters, or other service people, Americans tend to show their respect for the ideals of equality and individual dignity. They treat clerks and others as more or less equal to themselves, not as people who are clearly subordinate or inferior.

Tenant

A tenant's responsibilities are normally made explicit in the lease, or rental contract, the tenant signs. These responsibilities—paying a specified amount of rent by a specified date and properly caring for whatever appliances and furnishings the landlord provides—are the only things the tenant must do vis-a-vis the landlord. In effect, the landlord-tenant relationship is governed by the rule of law that is discussed in Chapter Five. The law in this case is the lease.

Particular tenants and landlords sometimes develop more personal relationships, of course.

Neighbor

A general rule among neighbors is to "mind your own business," that is, not to intrude in others' lives. Some neighborhoods are more friendly than others, meaning that more people in the neighborhood know each other and that the neighbors socialize with each other. However friendly the neighborhood, there is generally an expectation among Americans that neighbors will assist each other in times of emergency or very pressing need. It is considered reasonable to ask a neighbor to "keep an eye" on a house or apartment that is going to be vacant temporarily, as during a vacation. Newcomers to a neighborhood can take the initiative to invite neighbors for coffee, a pastry, and a get-acquainted conversation. Or they may themselves be invited by neighbors for a get-acquainted visit.

Neighbors in an apartment building may have virtually no interaction with each other.

Co-Worker

In general, co-workers treat each other with politeness and respect, regardless of their status vis-a-vis each other. The "boss" says "good morning" in a pleasant voice to the secretary and the file clerk; the latter smile and say "good morning" back. Co-workers help each other with job-related matters, and they try to avoid open expressions of displeasure or other negative feeling toward each other. Co-workers do not feel obligated to develop close relationships with each other, but they generally feel obligated to help make the emotional tone of the workplace pleasant for all who spend the day (or night) there. Many Americans have the idea that the workplace should have a kind of family atmosphere.

COURTESY

Among Americans, being courteous has a number of elements, as discussed below.

Acknowledging another person's presence or arrival, either verbally (if not with "hi!" then with "hello," "good morning," or some such greeting) or nonverbally, with a direct look, a nod, and a brief smile.

Participating in at least a bit of small talk with people in whose presence one expects to be for more than a few minutes.

Using vocabulary, tone of voice, and vocal volume no less respectful than that which one would use with peers at home. That is, courteous people do not "talk down" to others, giving them commands in an officious way or otherwise treating them as though they were inferior.

Saying "please" when making requests and "thank you" when requests are granted or services are performed. Americans consider it appropriate to say "please" and "thank you" to such people as waitresses, taxi drivers, hotel clerks, and dormitory maids.

Saying "You're welcome" in response to a "thank you."

Taking a place at the end of the line (what most people in the world call a "queue") and waiting patiently when a group of people have lined up for service, attention, or whatever.

SCHEDULES

Considerate people will be mindful of other people's domestic schedules, and will not telephone too early, too late, or during mealtime. Most Americans take breakfast between 7:00 and 9:00 a.m., lunch at noon or shortly thereafter, and an evening meal (called "dinner" in some parts of the country and "supper" in others) between 6:00 and 7:00 p.m. On Sundays, all meals may be somewhat later.

It is generally a good idea to make telephone calls to a person's home between the hours of 9:00 a.m. and 9:00 p.m. (except at mealtimes), unless there is reason to believe that everyone in the family will be awake before or after those hours.

GIFTS

Comparatively speaking, Americans give gifts on a relatively small number of occasions and to a relatively small circle of people. Since offering gifts to people who do not expect them can cause mutual embarrassment and can even lead to the suspicion that the gift-giver is seeking to influence the recipient in an inappropriate way, foreign visitors will want to be mindful of Americans' practices concerning gifts.

Generally, Americans give gifts to relatives and close friends. Frequently they give gifts (flowers, wine, or candy are common) to hostesses. They do not normally give gifts to teachers, business colleagues, or other people who might be in a position to grant or withhold favorable treatment (such as a good grade in a class or a contract for a sale). In fact, giving gifts to people who are in a position to grant or withhold favors can be construed as an improper effort to gain favor.

Christmas comes close to being a national gift-giving day in America. Except for adherents to non-Christian religions,

Americans exchange Christmas gifts with relatives, school-mates, and close friends. Other gift-giving occasions are days that are special to the recipient: birthdays, graduations, weddings, and childbirths. A "house-warming" gift is sometimes given to people who have moved into a new home.

Americans try to select a gift they believe the recipient could use or would enjoy. People are not expected to give expensive gifts unless they can readily afford them.

Americans commonly send a Christmas card to each of their acquaintances and sometimes to business colleagues as well.

SEX ROLES AND FRIENDSHIP

In many countries a friend must be a person of one's own sex. Most Americans, though, believe it is possible to have friends of the opposite sex. Americans do not generally assume that a male and female will participate in sexual activity if they are alone together. This is not to say that Americans see no sexual component in a male-female friendship. But they believe that the people involved are capable of showing the "restraint" and "maturity" necessary to avoid sexual interaction if sexual interaction is somehow inappropriate for the situation. Thus, a male and a female who are business colleagues might travel to a conference together without people assuming they have a sexual involvement with each other.

The next chapter explores the issue of male-female relationships in a bit more depth.

SUGGESTIONS FOR FOREIGN VISITORS

A number of specific suggestions have appeared in the preceding paragraphs. This chapter closes with some general ideas for foreign visitors who want to or are compelled to become involved in relationships with Americans.

The general advice is simple: Take the initiative, but go slowly.

"Take the initiative" because most Americans have their

lives organized and their time occupied before you come on the scene. For them it is easier to interact with other people who share their own language and culture than it is to interact with foreigners. Like most people in most countries, Americans will not usually seek out foreigners. Thus, those people here from abroad who want to get to know Americans will have to take the initiative in meeting people, starting conversations, and setting up opportunities for subsequent interactions.

"Go slowly" because it takes time, in America as anywhere else, to develop interpersonal relationships in which people know and trust each other and feel at ease in each other's company. Some foreign visitors become so lonely and make their need for companionship so plain to the Americans they meet that the Americans are frightened away. "He seemed absolutely desperate for someone to talk to," Americans might say after meeting a lonely foreign visitor. "I was afraid to get involved." Remember that Americans do not value dependence relationships the way many other people do. Rather, they fear them. Go slowly.

Have some conversation topics ready, so as not to be at a loss for something to say. (Remember that even brief lapses in conversation make Americans uneasy.) Most Americans are interested in topics or questions that have to do with cultural differences and with language. Make note of idiomatic terms or slang you hear and do not understand, and ask Americans what they mean. Keep in mind things you see Americans do that you are not sure you understand, and ask Americans about them. Tell them about amusing or mildly embarrassing experiences you have had in their country. Ask them about themselves—their families, their jobs, their travels, their interests. (But don't ask them questions about money!) If other things fail, talk about what to talk about. Explain what two people in your current situation would normally talk about if they were in your country, and ask what they would normally talk about here.

Find people or groups who share your interests. Millions of Americans belong to clubs or organizations centered on various hobbies, sports, and other avocational activities.

Finally, be persistent. Patient, but persistent. Not all of your efforts to establish rewarding social relationships with Americans will succeed. You are likely to have to try again and again until you meet a person or some people in whose company you find mutual enjoyment. When you do discover such people, you will have the best possible window on American culture.

CHAPTER 11

☆ ☆ ☆

Male-Female Relationship

If you ask several Arabs to list the characteristics of a good wife, the contents of their lists will be almost identical. Among other things, they will say the wife should be a virgin at the time of her marriage, that she should obey her husband and her mother-in-law, and that she should be devoted to raising her children.

But if you ask several Americans to list the characteristics of a good wife, the contents of their lists are likely to vary considerably.

In traditional or "high context" societies such as Arab ones, it is relatively easy to describe the patterns in male-female relationships. People in the society have agreed-upon ways in which young males and females can be together—or cannot be together, as the case may be. There are agreed-upon ideas about premarital sexual relations, appropriate wedding ceremonies, and proper behavior for husbands and for wives. Everyone knows what it means to be a good husband and a good wife.

With respect to male-female relationships, American society is exceedingly low-context. Almost nothing is agreed upon; everyone's list of the characteristics of a good wife or husband is different. The range of behaviors is remarkable. So foreign visitors have great difficulty understanding the male-female situation here. Indeed, Americans themselves have difficulty knowing how they should proceed in male-female relationships. They cannot be certain what to expect.

So it is not possible to describe here the behavior foreign visitors will see in the area of male-female relationships. Nevertheless, a few general comments might give visitors some context in which to understand what they see.

It is important to realize that people's ideas about appropriate behavior for women and for men are deeply-held, having been planted within them from a very early age. People tend to believe strongly that their own ideas on this subject are correct and that other ideas are wrong or somehow inferior. For example, men who believe that wives should not have jobs usually hold that belief very strongly. "No wife of mine is ever going to work," they will declare. People's ideas about what is proper in male-female relationships do not change easily (as those who enter cross-cultural marriages come to learn).

Foreign visitors usually find that American patterns in male-female relationships are different from the ones to which they are accustomed. If they themselves become involved with members of the opposite sex—as lovers, friends, or even careful observers—they are likely to have strong, negative reactions to some of what they see. At the very least, they will be confused and unsettled.

Besides these strongly-held ideas about what is and is not acceptable in male-female relationships, there is another obstacle to understanding these relationships when visiting another culture. That is stereotypes. The common stereotype of "loose" American women was mentioned in the preceding chapter. There are some other stereotypes that commonly impede foreigners' understanding of male-female relationships in America. We will look at them briefly and then consider some of the changes that are now taking place in male-female relationships in the United States.

STEREOTYPES ABOUT AMERICAN MEN AND WOMEN

Foreigners typically hold two stereotypes of American women. One, as has been said, is that they are loose—uninhibited about participating in sexual activity with a variety of men. The other common stereotype about American women is that they are domineering. "I wouldn't marry one of them," a Latin American graduate student said. "They try to rule men.

They argue and complain. I wouldn't want a wife like that."

A corresponding stereotype holds that American men are "weak," allowing themselves to be dominated by women.

Of course, Americans have their own stereotypes about sex roles and foreigners, or at least some types of foreigners. The principal stereotype that interferes with mutual understanding in this respect is that of the predatory foreign male. Many Americans—men and women both—have the idea that men from Southern Europe, Africa, Latin America, and the Middle East are persistently in pursuit of women with whom they can have sexual relationships. (This stereotype does not pertain to Asian men.)

As is often the case, these stereotypes have a germ of truth to them. One tall and handsome Middle Eastern graduate student said he had come to the States with the notion that women were readily available for sexual activities with people such as himself. Everything that happened to him during his first two years in the States confirmed his opinion, he said. A large number of women made themselves available to him.

After about two years, though, he began to realize that the women who were so available were not representative of the whole society. They were a certain type of person—insecure, socially marginal, apparently unable to find satisfactory relationships with American men. So they turned to foreign students. "Foreign student groupies," he called them. When he began to pursue women of other types, he found that they were not all ready to go to bed with him. His stereotype proved to be just that—an overgeneralized notion that applied in some cases but not in all.

CONTEMPORARY DEVELOPMENTS IN
MALE-FEMALE RELATIONSHIPS IN AMERICA

Whole books could be written (indeed, they have been written) about each of the topics touched on below. These brief comments are intended to give foreign visitors some context within which to place the impressions they are likely to get

about the way men and women relate to each other in the
United States.

Women's Liberation

The term "women's liberation" refers to a collection of
opinions and developments that, in general, seek to end discrimination against women—at least, discrimination that is
based on the notion that women are somehow inferior to men.
"Equal rights for women" is one of the movement's goals.
"Equal pay for equal work" is another. Adherents of the "wom-
en's liberation movement" (many of whom are men) urge that
school textbooks and teachers take note of women's contributions to history, science, and other fields. They argue for an end
to what they see as stereotyping of women on television and in
other media. They call for, and often get, female representation
on committees or other bodies whose decisions might affect
women's lives. They seek to "raise the consciousness" of all
Americans concerning what they consider to have been a pervasive, unfair, and unwarranted anti-female attitude in the society. Foreign visitors will hear a lot about the women's liberation movement. The topic is one about which many people
have strong feelings, whether they support the movement or
oppose it.

The themes underlying the women's liberation movement
are the same themes—individualism, independence, and equality—that underlie American society in general. Those who
favor "women's liberation" believe women have been unfairly
denied the rights and opportunities that, as American citizens,
they ought to have.

Those who oppose what they call "women's lib" see the
movement as subverting the social order, undermining family
life, and setting women against men in a way that is undesirable or even catastrophic.

Many of the specific changes discussed in the following
paragraphs are related to the women's liberation movement of
the mid-twentieth century United States.

Women working

As recently as 1960, only 33.3 percent of the American work force was female. By 1985, the percentage had risen to 54.7. More and more women, both single and married, are working outside their homes. Women's liberation no doubt has something to do with this new situation; difficult economic times have also contributed to the increase in female participation in the labor force.

Women are working not just in menial or clerical positions, as they once did, but in the professions and trades as well. It is more and more common to find female engineers, lawyers, doctors, dentists, and other professionals. Female housepainters, plumbers, and construction workers are not common, but they do exist. Fifteen years ago they did not.

The fact that more women are working has implications for male-female relationships. More women are earning money and are therefore in a position to assert their independence. Traditional female responsibilities in the areas of childcare and household maintenance are being reallocated. More and more men are doing things that only women, or mainly women, used to do. Visitors from male-dominated countries (and most other countries are more male-dominated than America is) may be shocked at first to see men shopping for groceries, washing clothes in laundromats (even folding women's underwear!), cooking in the kitchen, cleaning house, and taking care of children.

Single-parent families

As was mentioned in Chapter Six, the number of single-parent families in the United States is increasing markedly. According to U.S. census information based on families with children under 18 years of age, the number of families headed by a single parent has more than doubled in the past 20 years, from 10.1 per cent in 1965 to 22.2 per cent in 1985. A large portion of single-parent households are officially classified as "poor." Most single-parent households are headed by women.

Most of these women were once married, although an increasing number of American women are deliberately having children with no intention of marrying the child's father or anyone else.

Foreign visitors often take pity upon these single parents, viewing their situations as tragic. They assume that all these women—and any unmarried woman above the age of 25 or so—want to have a husband. The situations are probably "tragic" in some cases, but from the viewpoint of most Americans they are inevitable—indeed, in some ways preferable to the alternative of maintaining unhappy marriages—and quite acceptable.

Househusbands

Some couples have decided, for whatever reason, that the woman should be the one whose work supports the family financially, and the man should mind the house and the children. Men in that position are popularly called "househusbands." There are more and more of them in America.

Commuter couples

A contemporary American phenomenon foreign visitors have particular difficulty understanding and accepting is that of the commuter couple. In these couples, both work, one in one location and the other in a different, distant location. They maintain two households and they "commute" to see each other on weekends (if they live close enough together) or less often (if the distance between them is too great to make weekend travel feasible).

The commuter couple phenomenon seems to be an inevitable outcome of accepting the idea that a woman's career aspirations are no less important than a man's. If that idea is accepted, and at least some Americans accept it, then it will naturally happen that the marriage partners' careers will sometimes take them to separate places.

Unmarried couple households

As recently as 10 to 15 years ago, it was regarded as somewhat scandalous for an unmarried man and woman to "cohabit," or live together. Now, in many communities, such situations are accepted as a matter of course, by parents as well as others.

Blended families

Along with the growing divorce rate goes a growing number of remarriages and "blended" families—families composed of previously-married adults and the children of those previous marriages.

Sexual revolution

Academics and others argue about what a "sexual revolution" is and whether there has in fact been such a thing in the United States in the past 15 years or so. Those who believe there has been a sexual revolution point to a number of changes they think have taken place:

People, particularly younger ones, feel freer than they once did to talk about sex-related subjects. Masturbation, menstruation, impotence, frigidity, sex fantasies, sexual activities of various kinds, and the human sex organs are more likely to be talked or written about than they were 15 or 20 years ago.

The idea that women should be virgins at the time they marry apparently prevails among a diminishing portion of the population.

More young people are engaging in sexual intercourse before marriage.

Homosexuals (usually referred to as "gay" if they are male and "lesbian" if female) have become much less reluctant than they used to be to openly acknowledge their "sexual preferences." In some communities there has been legislation to protect gay people from discrimination in housing and jobs. Once again the American belief in individualism is reflected in legal efforts to protect a group of people whose behavior may not be approved of, but who are considered to have a right to behave as they wish.

On the other hand, concern that arose in the mid-1980s about the disease AIDS has lead at least some Americans to believe that promiscuous sexual behavior, whether homosexual or heterosexual, is potentially dangerous to participants and ought to be avoided.

Despite all the changes mentioned above, not everything has changed. Foreign visitors will still find individuals and communities where traditional ideas about male-female relationships hold sway. There are still many men and women who believe in premarital chastity (especially for women), marital fidelity, modesty about sexual functions, non-working wives, and male domination in families.

So, foreign visitors cannot safely make any assumptions about male-female relationships they may encounter or become involved in. They must observe carefully, ask questions, and take care not to let their own strongly-held ideas about male and female roles interfere with their understanding of what they see.

CHAPTER 12

☆ ☆ ☆

Sports and Recreation

Legend has it that Adolf Hitler got the idea for his mass rallies from observing the behavior of spectators at American college football games. Orchestrated by uniformed cheerleaders and roused by martial music, those spectators engaged in exuberant and emotional displays of support for their team. Hitler used similar devices to rouse support for the country he came to dominate.

Sports and recreation absorb a huge amount of Americans' emotion, as well as their time and, in some cases, money. "Sports" here refers to spectator sports, in which people watch others—mainly college and professional athletes—engage in competitive games. "Recreation" refers to leisure-time participation in athletics or other non-vocational activity.

SPORTS

Americans' interest in spectator sports seems excessive and even obsessive to many foreign visitors. Not all Americans are interested in sports, of course, but many are. And some seem interested in little else. Television networks spend millions of dollars arranging to telecast sports events, and are constantly searching for new ways (for example, using computer graphics and hiring glamorous announcers and commentators) to make their coverage more appealing. Publications about sports sell widely. In the United States, professional athletes can become national heroes. Some sports stars have become more widely recognized than any national leader other than the president. Some of them earn annual salaries in the millions of dollars.

What seems distinctive about American interest in sports is that it is not confined to particular social classes. People in all walks of life are represented among ardent sports fans. The collective audience for sports events is enormous.

Other observations foreign visitors commonly make about sports in America are discussed below.

Sports are associated with educational institutions in a way that is unique. Junior and senior high schools have coaches as faculty members, and school athletic teams compete with each other in an array of sports. Each team's entourage includes a marching band (especially associated with football, as Americans and Canadians call the game played with the oblong-shaped ball) and a group of cheerleaders. In some smaller American communities, high school athletics are a focal point of the townspeople's activities and conversations.

Nowhere else in the world are sports associated with colleges and universities in the way they are in the States. College sports, especially football, are conducted in an atmosphere of intense excitement and pageantry. Games between teams classified as "major football powers" attract nationwide television audiences that number in the millions. There is a whole industry built on the manufacture and sale of badges, pennants, T-shirts, blankets, hats, and countless other items bearing the totem and colors of various university athletic teams. Football and basketball coaches at major universities are paid higher salaries than the presidents of their institutions. Athletic department budgets are in the millions of dollars.

Said a recently-arrived foreign student in Iowa City, "It looks like the most important part of the University [of Iowa] is the football team. Maybe the team is the most important thing in the whole town."

Sports are a very frequent topic of conversation, especially (as noted earlier) among males. "Small talk" about sports is safe—interesting, but not too personal. Participants can display their knowledge of athletes and statistics without revealing anything considered private.

In some social circles, associating with athletes is a way to achieve social recognition. A person who knows a local sports hero personally, or who attends events where famous athletes are present, is considered by some people to have accomplished something worthwhile.

Expressions from sports are extraordinarily common in everyday American speech. Baseball is probably the source of more idiomatic expressions (examples: touch base; cover all the bases; two strikes against him) than any other sport. That fact disadvantages foreign visitors in communicating with Americans because most of them come from countries where baseball is not played.

Black Americans are heavily overrepresented in the major sports of baseball, football, and basketball. While Blacks comprise about 12 per cent of the country's total population, they make up well over half of most college and professional football and basketball teams. It is not unusual to see a basketball game in which all the players on the floor are black.

The women's liberation movement has brought considerable attention to women's athletics, so female athletes and games among female teams get more attention in the States than elsewhere.

The sport that is most popular in most parts of the world—soccer—is not well known in the United States. The most popular sports here are football and baseball, games that are not played in large numbers of countries.

Sports play such an important role in American life that the sociology of sports, sports medicine, and sports psychology have become respectable scholarly specializations. Perhaps scholars will someday be able to account for the popularity of sports in America, and for the various ways (some of which are given above) in which the role of sports in America differs from the role sports play in other societies.

Meanwhile, one practical suggestion: Foreign visitors—especially males—who plan to be in the United States for an extended period of time will enhance their ability to interact constructively with Americans if they take the trouble to learn about the sports teams that have followings in the local area. Knowing something about the games and the players, and about their importance in the natives' minds, improves the foreign visitor's chance of getting to know "average" Americans.

RECREATION

The word "recreation" brings to mind activities that are relaxing and enjoyable. Such activities as an evening walk around the neighborhood, a Sunday picnic with the family, and playing catch in the yard with the children seem relatively spontaneous and relaxing.

Much American recreational activity, however, seems to foreign visitors to be approached with a high degree of seriousness, planning, organization, and expense. Spontaneity and fun are absent, as far as the visitor can tell. "These crazy Americans!" a South American exclaimed on seeing yet another jogger go past her house in sub-freezing, winter weather. Many Americans jog every day, or play tennis, handball, racquetball, or bridge two or three times a week, or bowl every Thursday night, or have some other regularly scheduled recreation. They go on vacations, ski trips, and hunting or fishing expeditions that require weeks of planning and organizing. In the Americans' view, all these activities are generally fun and relaxing, or are worth the discomfort they may cause because they contribute to health and physical fitness.

Much American recreation is highly organized. There are classes, clubs, leagues, newsletters, contests, exhibitions, and conventions centered on hundreds of different recreational activities. People interested in astronomy, bird watching, cooking, dancing, ecology, fencing, gardening, hiking—and on and on—can find a group of like-minded people with whom to meet, learn, and practice or perform.

In America recreation is big business. Many common recreational activities require supplies and equipment that can be quite costly. Recreational vehicles (used for traveling and usually including provisions for sleeping, cooking, and bathing) can cost as much as $35,000. In 1984 Americans owned approximately 3,982,000 recreational vehicles, valued at about $7,733 million. Jogging shoes, hiking boots, fishing and camping supplies, cameras, telescopes, gourmet cookware, and bowling balls are not low-cost items. Beyond equipment, there is clothing. The fashion industry has successfully persuaded many Americans that they must be properly dressed for jogging, playing tennis, skiing, swimming, and so on. Fashionable outfits for these and other recreational activities can be surprisingly expensive.

A final point that astute foreign observers notice is the relationship between social class and certain recreational activities. The relationship is by no means invariable, and the element of geography complicates it. (For example, a relatively poor person who happens to live in the Colorado mountains may be able to afford skiing there, while an equally poor resident of a plains state could not afford to get to the mountains and pay for lodging there.) In general, though, golf and yachting are associated with wealthier people, tennis with better-educated people, and outdoor sports (camping, fishing, hunting, boating) with middle-class people. Those who bowl or square dance regularly are likely to represent the lower-middle class. Foreign observers will be able to find other examples of these relationships in whatever part of the United States they come to know.

CHAPTER 13

☆ ☆ ☆

Driving

"You can always tell when a car is being driven by a foreign student," said a Midwestern chief of police. "You don't have to be able to see the driver. They just don't drive the same way we do."

Foreigners' driving is noticeable anywhere. Driving entails not just the mechanical manipulations of the car—starting the engine, shifting gears, steering—but customary styles of driving as well. Driving customs vary from place to place, so foreigners' driving is often different from that of the natives.

Driving customs in America differ from one part of the country to another. In Pittsburgh, for example, a driver waiting at a red traffic light and wanting to turn left will race across the intersection in front of the oncoming cars just as the light turns green. Denver drivers will not do that; instead, they will wait until the oncoming traffic has passed and then they will make the left turn.

While there are marked regional differences in American driver behavior, there are some commonalities that foreign visitors who drive in the States will want to know about. After giving some general information about cars and driving in the United States, we will consider traffic laws, attitudes toward driving, and driving aids.

GENERAL INFORMATION

The ratio of motor vehicles to people in the United States is the highest in the world. Public transportation is generally not as accessible as it is in many other countries, and Americans tend to be too independent-minded to use common carriers anyway, so there are large numbers of cars. In 1985, 170,237,000 motor vehicles were licensed to operate in the United States. In many states the number of registered vehicles exceeded the number of licensed drivers.

Most Americans who have reached the age at which they can legally drive (the age is 16 in most states) have a driver's license. Females are as likely to drive as males.

Automobile accidents are not the grave social problem they are in some other countries, but they are still considered serious. In 1982 the rate at which fatal auto accidents occurred was 2.9 per 100 million vehicle miles driven, the lowest rate among countries for which data were available. By comparison, the rate was 3.4 in Finland and the United Kingdom, 4.8 in Japan, and 10.2 in Spain. A significant percentage of U.S. auto accidents involves drivers who have consumed enough alcohol to impair their judgment and reflexes. "Drunk driving" is considered a serious highway safety problem.

The U.S. road system is quite complex. State, county, and municipal authorities have responsibility for building, maintaining, and patrolling (with police) different highways and roads. Traffic laws vary somewhat from one jurisdiction to another, but there is general uniformity with respect to road signs, traffic lights, and the basic aspects of traffic engineering. (Some road signs are uniquely American; international signs are slowly being introduced.) Highways are kept as straight as possible. Except in the old cities on the East Coast, streets are generally laid out in a grid pattern unless geographical features make it difficult or impossible to adhere to that arrangement. Systems for naming and numbering streets vary.

TRAFFIC LAWS

Generally, American traffic laws cover the same subjects that traffic laws elsewhere cover: who can legally drive, minimum and maximum speeds, turning, parking, entering moving traffic, responding to emergency vehicles, vehicle maintenance, and so on. Drivers' licenses are issued by the separate states, usually through offices housed in county government buildings.

Traffic laws are enforced by state police on some roads, county sheriff's officers on others, and municipal police on still others. Police devote a significant portion of their time and effort to enforcing traffic laws. They issue what are called "traffic tickets," or simply "tickets," to violators. Drivers who get tickets normally have to pay a fine. In addition, most states have a "point system" whereby drivers are given points for each traffic offense. Drivers who accumulate a specified number of points will lose their driving privileges for a certain period of time.

Serious or repeated traffic violations can result in incarceration.

Trucks, motorcycles, and bicycles—all of which are wheeled vehicles that use the roads—are subject to traffic laws just as automobiles are.

ATTITUDES ABOUT DRIVING

Drivers' attitudes probably explain more of their behavior on the road than do the traffic laws. Foreigners driving in the U.S. of course need to know what the traffic laws say, but they will also want to understand the ideas that govern American drivers' behavior.

Attitudes toward traffic laws

Generally, Americans expect traffic laws to be enforced. They operate on the assumption that, at any time, a police officer might apprehend them if they violate the law. In general, American drivers take traffic laws seriously. A Southeast Asian high school teacher, in the States for advanced studies, learned how seriously when he tried to get an American driver's license. He failed the driving test twice before finally passing it. "They're so picky," he said of the driver's license examiners. "They kept saying I was breaking the laws." He had not stopped at some stop signs or given the required signals to indicate his intention to turn. In his own country such failures were quite acceptable.

Attitudes toward other drivers

Except for those—and there are many—who are looked down upon for being "aggressive" or "discourteous," American drivers tend to cooperate with each other. They are not likely to be constantly competing to see who can get the farthest the fastest. If they see another driver trying to enter the flow of traffic, for example, they are likely to move over (if there is a lane for doing so) or even slow down or stop (if they are not going too fast) to allow the other driver to enter. If they see that another driver wishes to change lanes in front of them, they are likely to allow it.

The ideal is the "courteous driver," who pays attention to other drivers and cooperates with them in what is conceived as a joint effort to keep the roads safe for everyone. Like other ideals, this one is violated. But it is the ideal nonetheless.

At the same time there is constant awareness of the concept of "right-of-way." The traffic laws try to make clear which driver has the right-of-way in each possible driving situation. For example, drivers going straight have the right-of-way over those heading in the opposite direction and wishing to turn left. Drivers without the right-of-way are expected to yield to those who have it.

Attitudes toward driving safety

Americans generally assume that individual drivers are responsible for their own safety and that of other drivers around them. Traffic accidents are usually considered to result from carelessness or mechanical failure, and not from "fate," "God's will," or other forces beyond human control. But "accidents do happen," the Americans will say, referring to the fact that an accident can occur through a random configuration of circumstances or as a result of factors that drivers could not reasonably be expected to foresee.

Attitudes toward pedestrians

Driver attitudes toward pedestrians vary from place to place. In some localities pedestrians are viewed as competitors for space on the roadway, and the burden is on the pedestrians to be wary. In other localities pedestrians are viewed as people whose wishes and apparent intentions deserve as much respect as those of other drivers.

One need only stand at an intersection and observe for a few minutes to see how local drivers and pedestrians view each other.

CHAPTER 14

☆ ☆ ☆

Shopping

"Things are so cheap here," a Latin American student's visiting mother-in-law exclaimed. "I've bought a TV, a VCR [videocassette recorder], some dresses and sweaters, perfume, and two hair dryers." She had also bought several pairs of pantyhose, her son-in-law confided, but she was too shy to mention that.

Whether they are planning a short stay or a long one, visitors to foreign countries often find they spend considerable time shopping. Short-term visitors such as the student's mother-in-law are often looking for souvenirs or for products that are considered bargains or "good buys" in the new country, or are things that cannot be purchased at home. Long-term visitors are shopping for the items they need to establish a household and get organized for daily life.

Shopping has common elements wherever it takes place. A buyer looks for a seller who is offering something the buyer wants or needs at a price the buyer can afford to pay. Sellers often advertise their wares in newspapers, on the radio or television, on posters, or elsewhere. Sellers use a variety of tactics to induce buyers to purchase from them at a price which leaves some profit.

Among the things foreigners often find unique about shopping in the United States are aspects of advertising, the pricing system, customer-clerk relationships, some of the tactics salespeople use to induce customers to buy from them, the procedures for buying and exchanging merchandise, and private sales. This chapter touches on each of these subjects, and then closes with some precautions for shoppers from abroad.

ADVERTISING

In the United States, advertising itself is a big business. Millions and millions of dollars are spent on television, radio, and printed messages to prospective consumers. Advertising firms do "market research" for their clients, testing out various "pitches" in the quest for ones that are effective.

From the viewpoint of American consumers, advertising functions to inform them about available products and services, as well as to encourage them to buy. From the viewpoint of visitors from abroad, though, advertising serves an additional function: it affords countless insights into American values, tastes, and standards. From American advertising, foreign visitors can gain some understanding of these and other aspects of American society:

American ideas about physical attractiveness in males and females,

American ideals concerning personal hygiene,

the emphasis Americans place on sex, speed, and technical sophistication,

the amount of faith Americans have in arguments that include specific numbers,

materialism in American society,

male-female relationships, both pre- and post-marital,

the attention Americans pay to the words of celebrities,

the characteristics of people who, in Americans' eyes, are considered "authorities," whose ideas or recommendations are persuasive, and

the sorts of things Americans find humorous.

By comparing advertising they see in the States to what they have seen at home, foreign visitors can gain understanding not just of American society, but of their own as well.

PRICING

With few exceptions, Americans are accustomed to fixed prices on merchandise they buy and sell. The usual exceptions are houses, automobiles, and sometimes major appliances such as refrigerators and washing machines. Another exception is at private sales, which are discussed below. Americans are not accustomed to bargaining over prices, and in fact usually feel quite uncomfortable with the idea.

Foreign visitors must realize that the price marked on an item does not include the sales tax that is added on as part of the payment. (Sales tax rates vary from one jurisdiction to another.)

Americans do not believe, as people from many cultures do, that a commercial transaction includes particular attention to the human relationships involved. They look for the item they want, decide whether they can afford the price marked on it, and, if they want to buy it, find a clerk or salesperson to take the money or do the paperwork for a credit-card purchase.

People who try to bargain for a lower price in a shop or store are likely to be considered either quite odd or startlingly aggressive.

CUSTOMER-CLERK RELATIONSHIPS

Some points about customer-clerk relationships have already been made. One is that clerks or salespeople are not normally looked down on or treated in a way that makes them seem less worthy than people in higher status occupations. In fact, foreign visitors are often startled by the degree of informality with which some salespeople treat them.

A final point that has already been made is that commercial transactions do not normally emphasize a personal relationship between the buyer and the seller. Both parties are considered to have a role to play, and they play their roles without necessarily making an effort to learn about each other's personal viewpoints or lives. This fact is quite plain to a customer who notices the mechanical smiles of clerks in many stores, and who hears again and again the refrains, "Have a nice day" and "Thank you for shopping at. . . ." The customer-clerk relationship may seem utterly dehumanized.

There are exceptions. Experienced sellers of automobiles, houses, major appliances, and other so-called "big-ticket items" will pay much attention to the buyer as an individual human being. People selling these products will operate on the assumption that they must become acquainted with their clients in order to help them select a product that will suit them and, at the same time, in order to understand what "pitches" are most likely to be effective with them. For example, an automobile salesman is likely to try to determine whether a particular customer will be more attracted to a high-performance sports car or to a "sensible," more conservative automobile. A person selling clothing may try to determine whether a particular customer is the type who will prefer something unusual or something that is popular.

Foreign visitors will notice striking differences in the degree to which clerks and salespeople are able to be helpful. Some are well informed about their products and can answer questions about them and about their employer's policies and procedures. Others seem to know little other than how to operate the cash register and fill out the forms involved in credit sales.

SALES TACTICS

Sales tactics, like advertising, reflect aspects of the basic assumptions and values that prevail in a country. By carefully listening to salespeople who are actively trying to sell them something, foreign visitors can enlarge their understanding of the way Americans perceive and think about things. Common sales tactics include trying to make the buyer feel sympathetic toward the seller; trying to make a male buyer feel that his masculinity is at issue when he is considering buying something, and that he will be less manly in some way should he not make the purchase; trying to make a female buyer believe that her attractiveness in the eyes of males will be enhanced by a particular purchase; placing a premium on a *rapid* decision to buy, with the idea that the opportunity to make the purchase will soon be gone; and trying to make the buyer believe that a particular purchase would be "wise," an example of the buyer's cleverness and foresight.

No doubt many of these tactics are used in some form or other in other countries. But the subtleties with which they are employed in the States are likely to be distinctive.

Two phenomena that startle some foreign visitors are those of the telephone solicitor and the door-to-door salesperson. Salespeople will telephone a person's home or just appear unannounced at the door and attempt to sell something to the occupant. Foreign visitors may need to realize they are not obligated to be courteous or attentive to such people. They need not be discourteous, but they can interrupt the salesperson, state that they are not interested, and hang up the telephone or close the door.

PROCEDURES FOR RETURNING AND EXCHANGING

As was said in Chapter Two, Americans consider it essential to have a written record of anything that is truly important. This is as true in commercial exchanges as it is in many other areas. Sellers routinely give—or will give if asked—receipts for purchases. Those receipts serve as evidence that the purchase was made, and most sellers will not entertain a request to return or exchange an item if the buyer cannot present the receipt for the original sale.

Most businesses will exchange a buyer's purchases for alternative items if the original one proves unsatisfactory. Some businesses will give cash refunds; others will not. Unless the buyer has the receipt, though, the business may give neither.

Guarantees and warranties come in the form of written documents that buyers must present if they are to get replacements or services that the guarantee or warranty provides.

PRIVATE SALES

Many foreign visitors are struck by the phenomenon of "garage sales" and "yard sales" in the States. Americans who want to sell a used car or other major item are likely to advertise it in the newspaper and try to sell it themselves, rather than go through a dealer. They will also sell small, used items such as pots and pans, clothing, tools, or books. They will go through their houses and collect items they no longer use and have a garage sale or yard sale in which they sort and mark the items they want to sell and set them out for display in the garage or the yard. They will advertise the sale, and then (typically) large numbers of people will come to their house and consider buying the items offered.

Foreign visitors who are going to live temporarily in the U.S. often find they can purchase many of the household items they need at garage or yard sales, where the prices are likely to be quite low and where bargaining over prices is acceptable.

PRECAUTIONS FOR SHOPPERS FROM ABROAD

Americans often quote the Latin axiom *caveat emptor* ("let the buyer beware") to convey their general conviction that people who buy things do so at some peril and must be vigilant against unwise use of their money. Two related axioms Americans use are "You get what you pay for" and "There's no free lunch." Both of these are interpreted to mean that purchases that seem like unbelievable bargains are usually not the bargains they appear to be.

These precautions are as valuable for foreign visitors as they are for Americans. So are the following suggestions:

Keep receipts for any purchase that might have to be returned or exchanged. Keep the written guarantees and warranties that come with many products.

Do not allow yourself to be rushed into making a purchase. Take your time. Think it over. Ask questions. Talk with other people who have bought the product or service you are considering and ask if they were satisfied.

Be aware that most salespeople will have some reaction to you because you are a foreigner. Some salespeople will have a beneficent attitude toward foreigners and will want to be particularly fair and helpful. Others will have a negative attitude and will see their interaction with a foreign customer as a chance to take advantage of someone's presumed ignorance.

Finally, remember that most businesses with merchandise displayed on shelves employ people, cameras, mirrors, and other devices to protect against shoplifting. People who believe it is easy to remove some item from a shelf, put it into a pocket, and leave the store without paying for it might quickly find themselves in trouble with the police. Many shoplifters are caught, and businesses generally do whatever they can to see that shoplifters are punished. Shoplifting is illegal and unwise.

CHAPTER 15

☆ ☆ ☆

Personal Hygiene

People's ideas about proper personal hygiene are deeply held. When they encounter a person who violates their ideas, they are likely to respond quickly and negatively. Foreign visitors who want to be able to interact constructively with Americans will therefore want to know what personal hygiene habits Americans are likely to consider appropriate.

American television commercials make clear what Americans consider ideal personal hygiene habits. The essential point is that Americans are taught that the odors a human body naturally produces—the odors of perspiration, oily hair, and breath—are unpleasant or even offensive. A person who follows what Americans consider good hygiene practices will seek to control those odors.

Body odors are controlled by bathing with soap, and mouth odors by brushing teeth with toothpaste. The popular conception is that people should bathe or shower at least once daily and brush their teeth at least that often, if not more frequently. They should use underarm deodorants to control perspiration odor and wash their hair however often is necessary to keep it from becoming oily.

In addition, people can use perfume, cologne, mouthwash, and other scented products to give themselves an odor that other people will presumably find pleasant. Whereas it used to be the case that only women used scented products after bathing, more and more men now do so. Perfumed soaps, scented aftershave lotions, and colognes intended for men (to give a "manly smell" that "women find attractive" or even "irresistible," as the commercials say) are more and more widely available.

The ideal person does not use "too much" of a scented product. "Too much" means that the scent is discernible more than three or four feet away from the person's body.

Most American women shave the hair from their underarms and from their lower legs (that is, from the knees downward). They wear varying amounts of makeup on their faces. "Too much makeup" is considered to make a woman look "cheap," that is, more or less like a prostitute presumably looks. What is "too much" varies from time to time and place to place. Foreign women wanting guidance on the amount of makeup that would be considered appropriate for them can pay attention to the amount of makeup worn by American women who are of an age and social status resembling their own.

Clothing, like bodies, should not emit unpleasant aromas. Clothing that has taken on the smell of the wearer's perspiration should be washed before it is worn again, according to the general American conception.

What has been said so far about Americans and personal hygiene describes their general notions on the subject and makes it all seem fairly simple. In truth, the matter is more complex. It is made more complex by (1) the variations one encounters with respect to personal hygiene, (2) Americans' attitudes toward talking about personal hygiene, (3) the stereotypes some Americans have about foreigners and their body odors, and (4) the psychological issues that arise when people are confronted with the idea that they ought to modify their hygiene practices. Each of these complications is discussed briefly here.

VARIATIONS

There are noticeable numbers of Americans who do not follow the practices described above. One variation is women who do not use makeup or perfumes. Makeup and perfume are not required for social acceptability, as long as the person is clean.

Another variation is people who do not use makeup or scented products but do not keep themselves clean and odor-free. There are various explanations for such behavior, including poverty, a wish to show independence or to protest against conventional practices, and a conviction that a more "natural" smell is somehow better. Foreign visitors will want to realize that the guidelines given at the outset of the chapter are those followed by what Americans call "polite company," that is, middle-class, conventional, "average" people. Those who fail to keep themselves clean are regarded as inconsiderate, rebellious, or worse. Foreign visitors who want to be in good stead with average Americans will want to adopt the personal hygiene practices that prevail in the country, even though, as the last section of this chapter says, doing so is not necessarily easy.

TALKING ABOUT HYGIENE

As Chapter Two pointed out, most Americans consider the subjects of body and breath odors to be too sensitive for discussion. They are "embarrassing." Most Americans will not tell other people that they have offensive breath or body smells.

But alert people can tell when their body odors are bothering others by the others' nonverbal reactions. In the presence of a person whose smells they dislike, Americans will keep their faces averted from the offending person, will sit or stand further away from the person than they normally sit or stand from those with whom they are interacting, and will draw the interaction to a close as quickly as possible so they can move away. The first two of these reactions—averting the face and backing away—will occur quite quickly, as soon as the American gets within a normal distance from the offending person and realizes that the person is giving off an unpleasant smell.

If the offending person is a foreign student, there may soon be a telephone call to the foreign student adviser's office. Most foreign student advisers have stories about calls from students or advisers in college residence halls. "I have this roommate" from such-and-such a place, the caller will begin. "He smells bad. But I just can't talk to him about it. Can you talk to him?"

STEREOTYPES ABOUT FOREIGNERS' BODY ODORS

"They smell bad," Americans sometimes say about about people from certain countries or world areas. "They must not use deodorants." Or "They don't take enough showers." Or, "It must be something they eat." Even if they have a sophisticated understanding of cultural differences, Americans are likely to respond negatively to what they regard as unpleasant body and breath odors emanating from a foreign person. Americans are, as some foreign visitors have said, "hung up" on body odor. They have strong, spontaneous reactions when they encounter it.

Interestingly, Americans themselves "smell bad," according to the stereotype the Japanese and some others have of them. What smells "good" and what smells "bad" turn out to be matters of personal and cultural experience.

PSYCHOLOGICAL ISSUES CONCERNING HYGIENE

Americans who encounter a foreigner who "smells bad" can be heard to ask, "Why doesn't he take a shower more often?" Or "Why doesn't he use some deodorant?" Similar questions (which are not asked in the offending person's presence): "Why does she wear so much makeup?" "Why doesn't she shave under her arms? That hair is so *ugly*."

Unfortunately, the matter is not so simple. The foreigners' attitudes about what constitutes proper hygiene practices are just as deeply held as the Americans' are. Many of them find the Americans' ideas unnatural. They may consider it unmanly for men to mask their natural odors, and unfeminine for women not to use a good deal of makeup. It is not easy for them to say, "Well, the Americans think I should take a shower every morning, shave under my arms, use deodorant, and launder my clothes more often. So I will, just to make them happy."

The question of the relationship between notions about personal hygiene and notions about masculinity, femininity, and integrity is beyond the scope of this book. But it is worth noting how complex the matter is because it causes a good deal of disharmony in intercultural relationships.

CHAPTER 16

☆ ☆ ☆

Getting Things
Done in Organizations

"Will you tell him?" my secretary has asked me many, many times. Usually the issue is with a Middle Eastern student. The secretary has told him that he cannot get some document he wants, or is not eligible for some privilege he is seeking. But he will not accept her answer, and he is becoming a bit unpleasant. "I think he needs to hear it from a man," the secretary explains.

I talk briefly with the student and explain that the secretary's answer is correct. The student cordially accepts the negative answer and departs. Meanwhile, the secretary is annoyed and insulted. That student is not likely to get her cheerful assistance in the future, even if he is asking for something she could readily supply.

One of the misconceptions many foreigners bring to the United States is that women cannot hold responsible positions in businesses and organizations. The idea that women can hold positions of authority is strange to them. They have been trained to believe that women are inferior or subordinate, and simply cannot have the ultimate authority in an important matter. In American organizations, though, it is increasingly common to find women in responsible posts. Many foreign student advisers, for example, are women.

Foreign visitors to the U.S. handicap themselves if they operate on the basis of assumptions about organizations that are not valid here. One of those invalid assumptions is that women do not matter. Four other common misconceptions are presented below. Then there is discussion of some characteristics that distinguish organizations in the States from those in many other places. Finally there are some guidelines for foreign visitors who must deal with organizations in the United States.

MISCONCEPTIONS

"I have to see the boss."

Many people come to the United States from countries where the only people in organizations who are considered capable of meeting a request, making a decision, or carrying out a procedure are the supervisors, the bosses, the "higher-ups." When they get to the States they will resort to a wide array of tactics to bypass the receptionist, the secretary, and the subordinate staff members in order to get into a room with the "boss," the one person they believe will be able to help them. Sometimes it is the case that only the boss can help, but far more often some subordinate employee can do so. The most common results of bypassing the subordinates to reach the boss are delays and irritation on the part of all the Americans involved. As will be discussed shortly, American organizations are normally based on the idea that people at all levels can accomplish constructive work.

"If I refuse to take 'no' for an answer I will eventually get my way."

In cultures where negotiation is widely used in dealings with organizations, or where organizational employees have wide latitude in making decisions, persistence might well be rewarded with an affirmative answer. In the States, though, organizational employees are typically bound by written rules that limit their discretion. Faced with a person who refuses to take "no" for an answer, they must persist in saying "no." Meanwhile they become increasingly annoyed and decreasingly likely to give any assistance whatever.

Most organization employees are incompetent.

In many countries it is believed that people get jobs in organizations on the basis of personal or political relationships and that the employees' main interest is in drawing their periodic pay rather than in working. Of course there are examples in the States of people getting jobs for reasons other than their interest in the work and their ability to perform their duties. And of course there are people who do not work hard. But the general conception among Americans is that people who work in organizations are capable of carrying out their assigned responsibilities and feel at least some pressure or obligation to do so.

Paperwork doesn't matter, or, I have to know somebody.

In many countries, impersonal procedures in organizations do not work, or work only very slowly. It is not enough to fill out an application form, for example. One must take the completed form personally to the boss or to some person one has a connection with and see to it that the application gets processed.

Not so in the United States. There are certainly cases in which knowing an employee of an organization can make things happen faster, and sometimes even make things happen that would not otherwise happen at all, but that is not generally the case. Generally, organizations operate in a context of explicit rules and procedures that everyone is expected to follow. The "rule of law," discussed in Chapter Five, prevails. Favoritism, or taking an action in someone's favor on the basis of a personal relationship, is considered bad practice and can even be punished.

CHARACTERISTICS OF AMERICAN ORGANIZATIONS

Many of the points to be made under this heading have already been mentioned, so this section can be brief.

Competence is the key to getting most jobs with U.S. organizations. In order to get jobs with most organizations, people have to have completed certain education or training programs, and often they have to have taken some sort of examination to demonstrate that they are prepared to do the work involved.

Efficiency is a primary concern of most organizations. Some are more efficient than others, but most strive to carry out their work as quickly as possible while not falling below certain standards of quality.

Foreign visitors are often struck by the relative efficiency of U.S. organizations. "You can get things done so easily here," they say. They notice that one telephone call can sometimes accomplish what at home might require two personal visits and three supporting documents.

The general idea of the *rule of law* is widely accepted. Organizations have written policies and procedures that are supposed to be followed no matter what people are involved. No doubt some individuals get favored treatment, but not in normal daily operations.

A graduate student from Brazil said that before he came to the States he supposed it would be impossible for him to get financial aid from any American university because he did not know anyone at any of them. He came to the States without aid. Later he filled out a scholarship application and submitted it to the appropriate university office, following the instructions printed on the form. He was awarded a scholarship even though he did not know anyone who worked in the financial aid office and even though he had not talked to anyone other than the secretary to whom he submitted the application form.

"I didn't believe that could happen," he said. "A friend in Brazil wrote to me a couple of months ago and asked if I could help him get some financial aid. I told him just to fill out the form and send it in. Things work that way here. I know he won't believe it. He'll think I have to help him, but in fact there's nothing I can do."

GUIDELINES FOR DEALING WITH U.S. ORGANIZATIONS

These guidelines follow from what appeared earlier in this chapter about American organizations and from what has been said in this book about Americans and individualism, equality, and the rule of law.

1. Be courteous to all employees, both male and female, even if they hold low positions.

2. Explain your request or question to the receptionist or secretary who answers the telephone or greets you at the office. Let that person decide what procedure you must follow or what other person you need to see.

3. If there is some procedure you must follow, ask about it so you understand it clearly. Find out what papers are involved, where the papers must be taken or sent, what steps are involved in the procedure, and how long the procedure can be expected to take.

4. Make a note of the names and telephone numbers of the people you deal with in case some delay or complication arises and you need to have further discussion with that person.

5. Should the procedure you are involved in take more time than you had been told it would (or a deadline has passed and you have not received a notification you expected, or you learn that a case similar to yours has already been processed), it is appropriate to "follow up" to see if there is some problem. In following up, take these steps:

    a. Begin with the lowest level person who is in a position to know about the procedure;

    b. In a pleasant, conversational way, explain who you are, what you have done, and why you are inquiring about the status of your case;

    c. Seek some statement about the projected completion date for your case;

    d. Again, note the names and telephone numbers of the people you talk to;

    e. Use care about showing anger. Anger might induce quicker action on your case, but it might also induce resentment, resistance, and further delays;

    f. Call on a higher person or an influential outsider only as a last resort, if you are convinced that the normal procedure is not working in your case.

6. Should the procedure work out in a way that is against your interests, ask what avenue for appeal is open to you. If there is a way to get a reconsideration, you will normally be told about it.

7. Keep in mind that in the States the telephone and mail service are used for many more things than they might be elsewhere. Inquiries and procedures that a foreigner might think require a personal visit may be taken care of in the U.S. by a telephone call or letter. It is quite acceptable to telephone an organization, say what you want, and ask for instructions about the most efficient way to proceed. Remember that Americans do not generally have the idea that they need a personal relationship with another person in order to have business dealings with them.

☆ ☆ ☆

Behavior in Public Places

When they are out in public—on sidewalks, in stores, restaurants, or in an audience—foreigners are constantly reminded that they are indeed foreigners. This is not just because the people around them differ in coloring, stature, and language, but also because the other people behave in unfamiliar ways. People's behavior in public places, like their behavior anywhere else, is subject to cultural influence. The American belief in equality, individuality, and progress are incorporated in the informal rules they follow in public places. Aspects of their communicative style are also evident when they are out in public.

COMMUNICATIVE STYLES

Voice volume

Words on a page cannot describe how loud sounds are. Suffice it to say that when they are in public places, Americans are generally louder than Germans or Malays, but not as loud as Nigerians or Brazilians. Of course, the volume at which people speak when they are in public places varies from one sort of public situation to another. The crowd at a baseball game will make more noise than the audience in a theater, for example. Patrons in a fast-food restaurant are likely to be noisier than those in a fashionable restaurant.

Foreign visitors who do not want to draw attention to themselves by their unusual behavior will want to note how loudly others around them in public places are talking, and adjust accordingly. Talking more softly than the Americans will cause no problems, but making more noise than they do will draw attention and, perhaps, adverse comment.

Touching

Americans' general aversion to touching others and being touched (discussed in Chapter Twenty-one) is clearly evident in public places. The "keep to the right" rule (see below) is one means of reducing the likelihood that strangers will have physical contact with each other.

Americans will rarely crowd onto a bus, train, or other conveyance the way Japanese and Mexicans are famous for doing. They will simply not enter situations where extensive and prolonged physical contact with strangers is unavoidable. Pushing one's way through a crowd is considered quite rude.

When they are in a situation where physical contact is unavoidable, Americans will typically try to draw in their shoulders and arms so as to minimize the amount of space they occupy. They will tolerate contact on the outsides of their arms when their arms are hanging straight down from their shoulders, but contacts with other parts of the body make them extremely anxious. When they are in a tightly crowded situation, such as a full elevator ("lift") or bus, they will generally stop talking or will talk only in very low voices. Their discomfort is easy to see.

In cases where they bump into another person or otherwise touch the other person inadvertently, they will quickly draw away and apologize, making clear that the touch was accidental. "Excuse me," they will say, or "Sorry."

Foreign visitors who violate Americans' notions concerning touching, in public places and elsewhere, are likely to be regarded as "pushy" or "aggressive."

RULES FOR BEHAVIOR IN PUBLIC PLACES

Keep to the right. When they are walking on sidewalks, in hallways, or on stairways—wherever groups of people are walking in two opposite directions—Americans stay on the right side. This enables them to pass each other without physical contact and to progress as quickly as possible.

Line up, and wait your turn. When they are in situations where a group of people want attention or service from someone, Americans line up (or "queue," as some people say). In the bank, at the theater box office, or at the university registrar's counter, the latest person to arrive will step to the end of the line and patiently (patiently unless it becomes clear that the service the people in the line are getting is slower than it ought to be) wait their turn. This behavior reflects their notion that all people are equal, in the sense that no one has the privilege of going directly to the front of a line. It also reflects their aversion to touching, which is much less likely to happen in a line than in a crowd jostling to get service.

People who do not go to the end of the line and wait their turn, but who instead go to the head of the line and try to push their way in front of others, will usually evoke a hostile reaction.

First-come, first-served. Related to the "line up" rule is the first-come, first-served rule. The general notion is that the person who arrives first gets attention first. Alternative notions, such as giving priority to older people or richer ones or males, do not normally occur to equality-minded Americans.

If several customers are standing up to a counter awaiting service, the clerk might ask, "Who's next?" An honest reply is expected.

Don't block the traffic. Generally, Americans give priority to people who are moving rather than to those who are stationary. A person who is in a moving crowd (on a sidewalk, for example) and who wishes to stop or to go more slowly than others is expected to move to the side or otherwise get out of the way of those who are continuing to move. It is considered inconsiderate to obstruct other people's paths.

Don't block the view. It is also deemed inconsiderate to obstruct another person's view when the person is trying to watch a public event, such as a parade, athletic contest, or theater performance. People toward the front of an audience or crowd are expected to try to position themselves so that people behind them can see. This rule can be interpreted as yet another manifestation of Americans' assumptions about equality and individualism.

A chapter on Americans' behavior in public places must discuss *cigarette smoking*. This chapter concludes with some words on that topic.

"I never thought much about when and where I smoked when I was at home," a German scholar said. "But here I notice that people look at me unpleasantly if I light a cigarette in a bus or in the restaurant. Several people have even asked me to put out my cigarette!"

In recent years an anti-smoking movement has made considerable headway in the United States. The results are many. Some states and localities have outlawed smoking in certain public places. Some restaurants, like airplanes, have areas designated for smokers and for non-smokers. Some localities prohibit smoking anywhere inside a restaurant. Many organizations have formulated rules about smoking, usually rules that specify where people can and cannot smoke. Non-smokers who feel discomfort in the presence of cigarette smoke often ask smokers (or *tell* them) to extinguish their cigarettes. Large numbers of Americans who formerly smoked have discontinued doing so, and vigorous campaigns in the public schools are aimed at discouraging young people from taking up the habit. People who do smoke are likely to postpone having a cigarette until they are in a situation where they can smoke without "polluting" the air around non-smokers.

Many foreign visitors, like the German scholar, come to the United States from countries where a higher portion of the people smoke and where what many Americans call the "right" of non-smokers to a smoke-free environment gets little or no attention. Such visitors, if they smoke without regard to local laws or non-smokers' sensitivities, are likely to give offense and be regarded as inconsiderate or worse.

Foreign visitors who smoke and who wish to avoid offend-

ing Americans will want to notice, before they light up, whether others in the group are smoking and, if they are, whether
they are confining themselves to a particular part of the room
or building. Asking those around them, "Do you mind if I
smoke?" is a good idea, and so is acceding to the wishes of those
who say they mind.

CHAPTER 18

☆ ☆ ☆

Studying

Many foreign students in the United States experience more difficulty and discomfort than necessary because they fail to understand and adapt to the behaviors Americans expect from college or university students. "I am sorry I came here," a recently-arrived Korean student said to me. "Many times I think about just quitting and going back home. It's not what I expected here. At home I was a good student. Here I don't know how to be a good student, and I can't make any friends."

Foreign students often feel lonely, isolated, misunderstood, and even abused because they do not understand the ways in which American students act in relationships with each other and with their teachers. This chapter discusses student-student and student-teacher relationships, roommate relationships, and the important topic of plagiarism.

STUDENT-STUDENT RELATIONSHIPS

Fellow students are independent people who may or may not wish to have conversations or begin relationships with classmates. It is always reasonable to address questions to fellow students and to ask their help with school-related matters. Of course, some will be more receptive to these requests than others.

Many foreign students are dismayed to find that American students do not help each other with their studies in the way students in their own countries do. Indeed, American students often seem to be competing with each other rather than cooperating. Foreign students who understand the degree to which

Americans have been taught to idealize self-reliance will understand much of the reason for the competition they see. Another part of the explanation is that many instructors in American schools assign final class grades "on the curve," meaning
that they award only a small, predetermined number of high
grades to the students in the class. When the instructor grades
on the curve, the students in the class are in fact competing
against each other to get one of the limited number of high
grades. (The alternative to grading on a curve is grading with an
absolute scale, in which case every student in a class could
possibly get a high grade.)

Another possible explanation for some American students'
reluctance to help others study is their fear of being accused of
cheating. See the remarks about plagiarism, below.

The degree to which American students pay attention to
foreign students, and the forms that attention takes, will vary
according to many factors. A primary one will be the amount of
experience the Americans have had in interacting with foreign
students or with other people who are different from themselves.

In most cases foreign students will find that they must
exercise some initiative if they want to have conversations or
relationships with American students. The latter will not generally approach foreign students with unsolicited offers of companionship or friendship.

The special case for foreign-U.S. roommate relationships is
discussed later in this chapter.

STUDENT-TEACHER RELATIONSHIPS

"My adviser wants me to call him by his first name," many
foreign graduate students in the U.S. have said. "I just can't do
it! It doesn't seem right. I have to show my respect."

On the other hand, professors have said of foreign students,
"They keep bowing and saying 'yes, sir, yes, sir.' I can hardly
stand it! I wish they'd stop being so polite and just say what
they have on their minds."

Differing ideas about formality and respect frequently

complicate relationships between American professors and students from abroad, especially Asian students (and most especially female Asian students). The professors generally prefer informal relationships (sometimes, but not always, including use of first names rather than of titles and family names) and minimal acknowledgment of status differences. Many foreign students are accustomed to more formal relationships and sometimes have difficulty bringing themselves to speak to their teachers at all, let alone address them by their given names.

The characteristics of student-teacher relationships on American campuses vary somewhat, depending on whether the students involved are undergraduate or graduate students, and depending on the size and nature of the school. Graduate students typically have more intense relationships with their professors than undergraduates do; at smaller schools student-teacher relationships are typically even less formal than they are at larger schools.

To say that student-teacher relationships are informal is not to say that there are no recognized status differences between the two groups. There are. But students may show their deference only in subtle ways, mainly in the vocabulary and tone of voice they use when speaking to teachers. Much of their behavior around teachers may seem to foreign students to be disrespectful. American students will eat in class, read newspapers, and assume quite informal postures. Teachers might not enjoy such behavior, but they tolerate it. Students, after all, are individuals who are entitled to decide for themselves how they are going to act.

American teachers generally expect students to ask them questions or even challenge what they say. Teachers do not generally assume they know all there is to know about a subject. Nor do they assume that they invariably explain things clearly. Students who want clarification or additional information are expected to ask for it during the class, just after class ends, or in the teacher's office at the times the teacher has announced as "office hours." Students who do not ask questions may be considered uninterested or uncommitted.

While most teachers welcome students' questions and comments about the material being covered in the course, they do *not* welcome student efforts to negotiate for higher grades. Teachers normally believe they have an acceptable system for determining grades, and, unless it seems possible that a mistake has been made, teachers respond very negatively to students who try to talk them into raising a grade. Some foreign students, particularly ones from countries where negotiating is a habit, severely damage their reputations in teachers' eyes by trying to bargain for better grades.

ROOMMATE RELATIONSHIPS

Foreign students may find themselves sharing quarters with American students, whether they deliberately sought out such an arrangement or the college housing office set it up for them. These arrangements can be enjoyable and educational or stressful and difficult, depending on a number of factors. One of the factors is the foreign student's knowledge of American culture. (Another factor is of course the American student's knowledge of the foreign student's culture, but American students do not generally enter roommate relationships with the idea that *they* will have to accommodate to a foreign student's way of seeing and thinking about things.)

Once again, what has already been said about Americans' values, thought patterns, and communicative style is consistent with what is said here about Americans and their relationships with roommates. It is well to remember that the ideas offered here are generalizations. Individual roommates will have their own personalities, and foreign students need to keep that fact in mind.

General comments

It is not possible to generalize about the assumptions American students make about the kinds of relationships they will have with their roommates. Some may be in quest of close friendship; others may simply want another person to share housing costs and may not want any more involvement with the roommate than a periodic reckoning of accounts. The remainder of this section is given to discussion of the *minimal expectations* Americans are likely to have about the behavior of their roommates.

Respect for privacy

Americans are likely to respond quite negatively if their roommates open or otherwise read their mail, listen in on their telephone or private conversations, enter their bedrooms uninvited, or ask questions they consider "personal." The Americans' notion of "privacy" generally means that their personal thoughts, their belongings (see the next paragraph), their relationships, and their living quarters are to be shared with others only if they themselves wish them to be shared.

Respect for "private property"

Americans generally conceive of their material possessions as being, in a sense, extensions of themselves. Just as they do not readily share their innermost ideas with others, they generally do not share their possessions with others until agreements about the terms of the sharing have been reached. Roommates, whether foreign or American, do not share their clothing, toilet goods, appliances, books, and other possessions without prior agreement. You should therefore not borrow, use, or even touch a roommate's possessions without permission.

Sharing the burdens

Americans will generally expect an even sharing of duties such as cleaning, shopping, shoveling snow, and paying bills. If there are two roommates, then the sharing is expected to be, as the Americans often say, "fifty-fifty."

Being considerate

Most Americans will extend consideration, and will expect consideration from their roommates, concerning noise levels, smoking, and schedules for using joint facilities. If one roommate wants to use the shared quarters for a party on Friday night, for example, that roommate is expected to confer with the other to make sure that some conflicting event or activity is not planned. Roommates are expected to take messages for each other should telephone calls or visitors come in the other's absence.

Being direct

Americans are likely to expect their roommates to be direct and assertive in expressing their preferences and in making it known when they are inconvenienced or otherwise negatively affected by something the American is doing. "How would I know he didn't like the stereo on so loud?" an American might ask. "He never said anything to me about it."

For some elaboration about and suggestions for benefitting from relationships with American roommates, see my *Learning with Your Foreign Roommate* (Iowa City: University of Iowa, Office of International Education and Services, 1982).

PLAGIARISM

To plagiarize is to represent someone else's academic work—in the form of writing or ideas—as one's own. The Americans' belief in the value of the individual and the sanctity of the individual's property extends to ideas. Ideas belong to people; they are a form of property. Scholars' writings and ideas are considered their property. Students and other scholars are not supposed to use those ideas in their own writing without acknowledging where the ideas came from. To leave out the acknowledgment and thereby convey the impression that another's words are one's own is "plagiarism."

Foreign students are sometimes accused of plagiarizing the

works of other people. It is probably the case that much of the plagiarism foreign students commit (usually by copying the words of another writer into a paper they themselves are writing and failing to include a footnote saying who originally wrote the words) is committed out of misunderstanding rather than out of dishonesty. To American scholars the notion of "intellectual property" is perfectly clear and sensible. It is obvious to them when an idea has been "stolen." And stealing ideas is a cardinal sin in the American academic world.

Many foreign students do not share the Americans' conceptions about individuality, private property, and the ownership of ideas. They see no wrong in copying relevant, well-expressed ideas into a paper they are writing. But their faculty will see it as quite wrong, and foreign students need to know that and behave accordingly.

CHAPTER 19

☆ ☆ ☆

Business

A female colleague who formerly worked for an oil company in the Southwestern United States told this story:

One summer the president of my company had a party at his house. The president is 6 feet, 5 inches (196 cm.) tall, has golden blond hair, and is sometimes compared to a polar bear.

At the party, the executive vice presidents (aged 35 to 45) bet me that I couldn't throw the president into the swimming pool. I am 5 feet, 1 inch (155 cm.) tall. I accepted the bet.

I took a drink to the president and lured him to the edge of the pool. I explained the bet to him. He was most sympathetic to my situation. To have refused the bet would have shown either timidity (a horrible affliction in a high-risk business) or that I wouldn't "play" with the "boys"—a rejection of their offer of equality. The president told me to put my hand on his back, count to 3, and push, saying he would jump in. I did. As I pushed, he turned to me, smiled, picked me up and tossed me into the center of the pool. When I surfaced, I saw the vice presidents throwing the president in. (It took three of them.) By the ' nd of the afternoon everyone, including the hostess, had been thrown into the pool.

This story illustrates at least three aspects of American business life that people from abroad notice very quickly. The first is one that may not seem to be a matter of culture, but probably is. American executives (if they are male) are likely to be *tall*. Studies done at the University of Pittsburgh have shown a clear correlation between a male executive's height and his status in his organization. Taller men are more likely to get to higher positions in their organizations and to be paid higher salaries. Foreigners who meet high-level American executives are likely to be dealing with tall males. Tallness is associated in many people's minds with the strength, power, and competitiveness that are idealized in American business.

Another characteristic foreigners notice is *informality*. They may not witness a president being tossed into a swimming pool by the vice presidents, but they are likely to see and hear much more informal behavior than they would among colleagues at home. American businesspeople, at least as much as so-called average Americans and probably more so, address other people by their first names, make jokes, and use a vocabulary and tone of voice suitable for informal relationships. They may dress relatively casually; men may remove their coats and loosen their neckties if they are in a long meeting. Because they are likely to equate formality with discomfort, they are likely to urge others to "relax" during their dealings.

Finally, my colleague's story makes clear that there are *women* in American executive circles. They are still in a minority, and they encounter many obstacles in their efforts to advance, but they hold responsible positions in a growing number of organizations. Visiting businessmen are well advised to be ready for the possibility that they will be interacting with a woman who has expertise and authority they assumed only a man could have.

They may appear informal and relaxed, but American executives generally *work hard*. They will devote long hours—as many as 16 or 18 per day—to their jobs. They may consider their work to be more important to them than family matters and social relations. Americans use the term "workaholic" to describe a person addicted to work, one who spends as much time as possible on the job and seems to think of little else. Workaholics are by no means rare in the American business world.

American executives often embarrass their foreign counterparts by doing manual work or by doing tasks that elsewhere would be done only by lower status people—tasks such as serving coffee, rearranging the furniture in a meeting room, or taking out a calculator to figure out a problem that came up during a meeting.

Punctuality and schedules are important. Meetings and appointments ideally begin and end "on schedule." The topic that is supposed to be treated during the meeting or appointment is generally expected to be covered by the scheduled ending time. Delays cause frustration. Getting behind schedule is likely to be considered an example of bad management.

In keeping with their notions about the importance of using time wisely and getting the job done, American executives generally want to *"get right down to business."* They do not want to "waste time" with "formalities" or with long, preliminary discussions. In fact, they are usually quite uncomfortable with purely social interactions while they are working. Americans generally have no particular interest in getting personally acquainted with the people with whom they deal. As long as they believe the other party is trustworthy in business dealings and has the ability to deliver whatever product or service is being discussed, the Americans will proceed in an *impersonal* manner. They value *decisiveness* and *efficiency*. Concerns about human relations are lower down in their scale of priorities. Western Europeans are likely to carry on in about the same way, but people from most other parts of the world are likely to find the American approach cold or otherwise uncomfortable.

Even when they seem to be socializing, as at a dinner or reception with business colleagues, their main purpose is more likely to be discussing business than becoming personally acquainted with other people.

American businesspeople, probably even more noticeably than Americans in general, prefer to think and analyze in *quantitative terms.* They want "hard data" and "facts and figures" when they are analyzing a business situation and trying to make a decision. The assumption is that wise decisions are made on the basis of "objective" information uncontaminated by considerations of personal feelings, social relations, or political advantage.

American executives frequently use the term "bottom

line," which refers to the final entry in an accounting statement. They want the statement to show a profit. Nothing else is as important. The purpose of a business is to make a profit, and executives are evaluated with reference to their contribution to the company's financial standing.

The *written word is supremely important* to American businesspeople. They make notes about conversations, keep files on their various projects, and record the "minutes" of meetings. The contract or the agreement must be written down in order to be taken seriously. And every written word is important. It must be the correct word, the one that makes clearest what each party's rights and obligations are.

To Americans in business, then, it seems perfectly natural to consult *lawyers* about contracts and agreements. Lawyers are trained to select the proper words and to correctly interpret documents. Americans have difficulty understanding that people from elsewhere might consider oral agreements to be adequate. Businesspeople from abroad might feel insulted by the Americans' insistence on having written agreements, viewing the Americans' attitude as an indication of distrust.

Meetings are a common phenomenon in the business world, but what actually happens in meetings varies greatly, not just from country to country but from organization to organization. Meetings can have a variety of purposes—sharing information, giving instructions, heightening enthusiasm and dedication, discussing issues and problems, suggesting solutions, and no doubt others. The mix of these various purposes probably varies in different countries and different organizations. Americans like to know explicitly what the purpose of any given meeting is. "What's the point of this meeting?" they may ask.

The leader's role in meetings varies. The leader might be the one who opens the meeting, does all the talking, and then dismisses those who have attended. Or the leader may play the role of a moderator, opening the meeting and then allowing others to discuss matters and make decisions.

The role of those attending the meeting differs too. They may be expected to sit quietly and listen, or to offer suggestions or comments, or even to challenge ideas others put forth.

In the ideal American meeting, the leader encourages active participation of all those who might have ideas to contribute. The people at the meeting offer ideas and information intended to help illuminate the subject under discussion. They may openly and bluntly disagree with each other. Witnessing such meetings can shock foreigners who are accustomed to more formal, hierarchical arrangements, where the leader firmly controls what takes place and participants either remain silent or mask any disagreement they might have with what others say.

In American meetings, issues are often resolved by means of a vote. "The majority rules," Americans often say—not just in this context but in others too. The practice of voting in meetings might disconcert foreigners who are accustomed to a system in which decisions must be unanimous, or one in which the people in authority are the ones who make the decisions.

So far we have been talking about "business" as it relates to encounters between American executives and executives from abroad. Much international business activity involves only executives. They meet, explore possible business relationships, negotiate contracts, then return to their daily routines in their own offices.

Some foreign executives stay longer in the States and have the opportunity to observe other aspects of American business besides executives' behavior. Whether they are continuing to work with the executives or are supervising American workers, they will have to accommodate themselves to the workings of the organization's lower levels. The better they understand how the organization is set up and how it operates, the more effective they can be. This chapter concludes with comments about a few aspects of American business operations that stand out in the minds of many foreign visitors.

Americans' notions about equality strongly influence what happens throughout business organizations. Although people at various levels are quite aware of the status differences among them, they may not display superiority or inferiority in open ways. Rank-conscious foreigners are made to feel uneasy by the relatively relaxed and informal interactions they will see between lower status employees and those with higher status.

Another manifestation of the equality assumption is the prevalence of written rules and procedures. If people are considered equal, then they must be treated fairly or "impartially," that is, without reference to their own particular personalities. Fairness is best assured, in the typical American view, if there are written rules and procedures that apply to everyone equally. So there will be written procedures for hiring, training, evaluating, disciplining, and terminating employees. There will be written procedures for handling employee complaints. There are job descriptions, safety rules, and rules for taking "breaks" (rest periods) from work. Great stress is placed on carrying out the written procedures completely and correctly.

Foreign visitors are likely to think the constraints Americans impose on themselves by means of their rules are excessive, especially if labor union rules are added to those of the company.

Foreign visitors may see more *employee turnover* than they are accustomed to. America is still a more mobile society than most (the rate of mobility may have slowed recently), so people change jobs relatively readily. It is unusual to find a strong sense of company loyalty at the lower ranks of a business. People have their jobs to earn a living, and in many ways it does not matter to them just where that living comes from. They do what they are supposed to do (according to a written job description, usually), collect their pay, and go home. Supervisors are often seeking ways to enhance employee allegiance to the company, in the belief that employees who are more "loyal" will be more productive.

Finally, there is the matter of American workers' attitudes toward foreign executives. As has already been pointed out, Americans generally know little about other countries. They generally assume their own country is superior. While they may know full well that a foreign executive outranks them, they may still deem themselves superior in some way simply because they are Americans.

CHAPTER 20

☆ ☆ ☆

Nonverbal Communication

"You shouldn't have your office arranged like this," a Nigerian student declared to me. "You should have it so your desk is between you and the person you are talking to."

"You shouldn't have your furniture this way," a Chinese scholar told me. "You should not have your back to the door when you are at your desk. It brings bad luck. You should be facing the door."

"I like the way you have your office set up," a Canadian student observed. "It's nice and informal. You don't have a desk between yourself and the person you are talking to, so the person feels more at ease."

Furniture arrangements are just one aspect of a large topic, "nonverbal communication." The types and relative positions of the furniture in an office or a home convey messages to people about such topics as degrees of formality and concern with social status. And, as the examples above make clear, a given arrangement conveys different messages to different people.

Body smells, volume of voice, clothing styles, and attention to punctuality—these are among the many other aspects of human behavior that come under the heading of nonverbal communication. The subject is large, complex, and not very well understood. It seems clear, though, that much communication among human beings takes place on the nonverbal level. It also seems clear that many aspects of nonverbal communication are heavily influenced by culture.

Finally, it is clear that much discomfort in intercultural situations stems from differences in nonverbal communication

140

habits. People in cross-cultural interactions are often uncomfortable for reasons they cannot specify. Something seems wrong, but they are not sure what it is. Often what is wrong is that the other person's nonverbal behavior does not fit what one expects or is accustomed to. The result of this discomfort is often negative judgments about the other person as an individual or about the group the other person represents.

So, some understanding of nonverbal communication is essential for people who want to get along constructively in another culture. This chapter talks about several aspects of nonverbal communication and makes some observations about typical (but, remember, not universal) American nonverbal behavior.

ASPECTS OF NONVERBAL BEHAVIOR

With respect to *general appearance and dress*, generalizations about Americans (or any other large and diverse group) are scarcely possible. Suffice it to say that Americans, like people elsewhere, have ideas about which clothing styles are attractive and unattractive, or appropriate and inappropriate for any given setting. These ideas change from time to time because they are subject to fads and fashions. So do ideas about hairstyles, cosmetics, and jewelry, all of which are aspects of nonverbal behavior. Foreigners anywhere usually stand out because their hairstyles, clothing (including shoes), and use of cosmetics make them appear different from the natives.

Body movements are an important aspect of nonverbal communication. Many foreign visitors think they see a characteristic "American walk," in which the walker moves at a rapid pace, holds the chest forward, and swings the arms vigorously. All of this creates the impression in some foreigners' minds that the American takes up more space than he actually does, and that he is arrogant.

With respect to *movements accompanying their talk*, Americans consider what can be called "moderate" gesturing appropriate. They use hand and arm motions to add emphasis or clarity to what they are saying, but they will not generally use a gesture in which the elbows go above the level of the shoulder. (Exceptions: waving hello or goodbye, voting by show of hands, and trying to get the teacher's attention in a class.) People whose elbows rise above their shoulders while they are talking are considered to be "waving their arms," which is taken as a symptom of excessive emotionalism and perhaps even of anger. In Americans' eyes, Italians, Greeks, and some Latin Americans are likely to be considered "too emotional" or "hot-tempered" because of the vigorous gestures that often accompany their talk.

On the other hand, people who keep their hands and arms still or very close to their bodies while they talk are likely to be regarded as "too stiff," "too formal," "up-tight," or "too polite." Americans often think of Chinese and Japanese people, particularly females, in this way.

In most societies there are *standard gestures* for certain everyday situations: greetings (a gesture that goes with "hello!"), leave-takings (a gesture with "goodbye"), summoning, head movements to signify agreement or disagreement, and counting and showing numbers with the fingers. There are also certain gestures that are considered obscene in the sense that they refer disrespectfully to body functions, usually sexual ones. It takes more space than is available here to describe the gestures Americans typically use for each of these situations. The easiest way for foreign visitors to learn them is to ask an American for a demonstration.

Foreign visitors will want to be aware that Americans are likely to overlook or misunderstand gestures that the foreigners use and Americans do not. For example, people from certain parts of India typically move their heads in a sort of figure-eight motion when they are listening to someone talk. To the Indians this gesture means "I am listening, I understand." Americans do not have a similar gesture. The Indian head movement is not the same as the one Americans use to indicate agreement (the head goes up and down) or disagreement (the head goes side to side). It is something else. It is likely to suggest to Americans that the Indian has a sore neck, a tight muscle that he is trying to loosen by moving his head around.

When conversing with an Indian who seems to have a sore neck, the American may become so preoccupied with the "strange" head movements that he loses all track of the conversation. This is one of the dangers of differences in nonverbal behavior. "Strange" gestures and postures can be extremely distracting.

People who are particularly interested in the topic of gestures are urged to read a book called *Gestures*, by social psychologist Desmond Morris. The bibliography at the end of this book has more information about Morris's work.

Social scientists debate whether there are certain *facial expressions* that mean the same thing to people everywhere. Without entering that debate, we can say that Americans generally permit more emotion to show on their faces than many Asians typically do, but less than Latins or southern Europeans. Foreign visitors who are unsure of the meaning of an American's facial expression (remember, don't assume those expressions mean the same thing they mean at home!) can ask about it.

Smiling is a facial expression that causes particular difficulty. Americans associate smiling with happiness, cheerfulness, and amusement. They rarely realize that many Asians will smile (and even "giggle" or laugh softly) when they are confused or embarrassed. "I don't know why she kept smiling," an American might say. "I didn't see anything funny!"

Eye contact is an aspect of nonverbal behavior that is especially complex, subtle, and important. The issue is simple: when you are talking to another person, where do you direct your eyes? There are marked cultural variations in people's answers to that question. Americans are trained to distrust people who do not "look them in the eye" when talking with them. The fact is that Americans do not gaze continually into the eyes of people they are talking to unless they share an intense romantic relationship. What they do, rather, is make eye contact when they begin to speak, then look away, and periodically look again into the eyes of the person they are talking to. They look at the other person's eyes when they reach the end of a sentence or a point in the conversation where they are prepared to give the other person a turn to speak.

When listening to another person, Americans will look for longer periods into the other person's eyes, but will still look away from time to time.

Foreign visitors can watch pairs of Americans who are talking and take note of what they do with their eyes.

Visitors whose habit it is *not* to look into the eyes of a person they are talking to will be able to tell, if they are observant, that Americans are uncomfortable around them. So will those whose habit it is to look for longer periods or stare into the eyes of people with whom they are talking. Americans feel that something is wrong when the person they are talking with does not look at them in the way described above.

Another aspect of nonverbal behavior that culture strongly influences has to do with *space and distance*. It can be amusing to watch a conversation between an American and someone from a culture where habits concerning "conversational distance" are different. If an American is talking to a Greek, a Latin, or an Arab, the American is likely to keep backing away because the other person is likely to keep getting "too close." On the other hand, if the conversation partner is Japanese, the American will keep trying to get closer because the Japanese insists on standing "too far away." Conversation partners in these situations might move clear across the room as one gets closer and the other backs away, each trying to maintain a "normal" conversational distance. All the while, both people are vaguely uncomfortable and are likely to be making negative judgments about each other. "They're cold and unfeeling," Latin Americans might say of North Americans who keep moving away. "They are pushy and overbearing," Japanese might say.

With respect to *touching*, the questions are: Who touches whom? Where (that is, on what part or parts of the body)? Under what circumstances? What kind of touching (patting, rubbing, hugging)? Dean Barnlund made an interesting comparison of touching among Japanese and among Americans. (See *Public and Private Self in Japan and the United States*, published in 1975 by Simul Press, Tokyo.) He asked his subjects (who were university students) to show on a diagram what parts of their bodies had been touched since they were 14 years of age by their fathers, their mothers, friends of the same sex, and friends of the opposite sex. He found striking contrasts between the two groups. The least-touched American remembered being touched more than the most-touched Japanese did. Some Japanese could not recall having been touched by anyone since age 14.

A comparison between Americans and Latin Americans, Arabs, or southern Europeans would no doubt show that Americans, while they touch each other more than Japanese typically do, touch less often than people from some other cultures.

Of course, habits and preferences concerning touching vary not just by culture, but by individual and by situation. Some individuals like to touch and be touched more than other individuals do. Careful observation can reveal a particular individual's preferences in this respect. Status differences also affect touching behavior. In general, higher status people are freer to touch lower status people than vice-versa.

People's notions about *time* vary by culture. Americans conceive of time as a kind of line from the past through the present to the future. They do not think of time as cyclical. Some typical American ideas about time—about using it wisely, and being prompt—have already been discussed.

The final aspect of nonverbal behavior to be mentioned here is that of *silence*. Except in the presence of people they know fairly well, Americans are quite uncomfortable with periods of silence in a conversation. If conversation lapses more than a few seconds, alert foreign visitors will notice Americans quickly devising something to say. Almost any comment, in their view, is preferable to silence. A silence of 10 or 15 seconds will bring nervous perspiration to many Americans' brows.

SUGGESTIONS FOR DEALING WITH DIFFERENCES IN NONVERBAL BEHAVIOR

Foreign visitors cannot expect to learn and employ all of the Americans' nonverbal communication habits, but there are some things they can do to minimize the negative effects of differences in these habits:

1. Be aware of the wide range of human actions and reactions that come under the label "nonverbal communication," and realize that such behavior is largely culturally based.

2. Learn as much as possible about American nonverbal communication habits, and practice doing things that way. Remember that there is no reason to expect them to adopt your way while you are in their country.

3. Do not develop an exaggerated idea about the effects of differences in nonverbal communication. While the differences are pervasive and important, they are not the only thing happening in any intercultural encounter. What the other person is actually saying may offer an accurate guide to the message the person wants to convey. Each situation provides its own clues about what other people want and expect.

4. Try to avoid interpreting what others mean and evaluating their behavior based on your own ideas about appropriate nonverbal behavior. For example, if you are accustomed to standing closer to conversation partners than Americans generally are, be careful not to interpret the Americans' preference for a greater space between you as a sign of coldness, dislike, or disrespect. Such an interpretation might make sense at home, but not in the United States. The more you can learn about how Americans interpret each other's nonverbal behavior, the more constructively you will be able to interact with them.

PART III

★ ★ ★

Coping with Cultural Differences

Some people find cultural differences interesting and exciting. They are mentally and physically stimulated by encounters with people from other cultures, and they want more.

Other people, though, do not have that reaction. In the presence of people from different cultures they feel discomfort, confusion, and anxiety. They have a strong tendency to judge or evaluate other people and to reach negative conclusions about them.

Surely people of the first type are more likely to have constructive experiences with people from other cultures than are those of the second type. Can anything be done to help people react more constructively than they might otherwise? Part III is based on the assumption that some things can be done.

Chapter Twenty-one offers some *ideas* about intercultural relationships and adjusting to new cultures. Chapter Twenty-two suggests some *activities* that are intended to help foreign visitors understand their own ideas about intercultural encounters and also understand Americans better.

CHAPTER 21

☆ ☆ ☆

Some Helpful Ideas

Two Japanese businessmen are assigned to work in the States. They are just a year apart in age. Both work for the same large automobile corporation, both are trained as mechanical engineers, and both are sent to the same American city to help test their company's cars under mountain and winter driving conditions.

One is miserable in the States, and the other has an interesting and enjoyable time. What accounts for the difference? It is not possible to say for certain, but it is clear that the *ideas* and *attitudes* people bring to the States from other countries—as well as their *knowledge* of American society and culture—have a strong influence on the nature of the experience they have. One of the Japanese engineers, it is safe to say, had some ideas that the other one did not have. This chapter presents an assortment of ideas that can help visitors to the United States respond positively and constructively to their experience.

EXPECTATIONS

Be aware that your reactions to your experience in the States have as much to do with *your expectations* as they do with what actually happens to you. When you find yourself disturbed or upset about the Americans, ask yourself, "What did I expect? Why did I expect it? Had I known more, would I have expected what I actually experienced?" Unrealistic expectations create much unhappiness for foreign visitors. That graduate student in Pittsburgh who could not find an apartment building inhabited by airline stewardesses had some unrealistic expectations, as he came to realize after he talked with some other students who had been in this country longer.

PERSONALITY CHARACTERISTICS

Scholars and researchers have attempted to determine what personality characteristics go along with success in intercultural experiences. Their findings have often been unclear or inconclusive. But three characteristics recur in their reports: patience, a sense of humor, and tolerance for ambiguity.

Patience, of course, is the ability to remain calm even when things do not go as one wants them to, or hopes they will, or has even been assured they will. Impatience sometimes brings improvements in relations with other people, but usually it does not. It is usually counterproductive.

A person with a sense of humor is less likely to take things too seriously and more ready to see the humor in her own reactions than is a humorless person. The value of a sense of humor in intercultural relations is difficult to overestimate.

"Tolerance for ambiguity" is a more difficult concept than patience or sense of humor. Foreigners often find themselves in situations that are, to them, ambiguous. That is, they do not know what is happening in the situation. Perhaps they do not understand the local language well enough, or they do not know how some system or organization works, or they cannot determine different people's roles in what is going on, or they do not know what assumptions the natives in the situation are making. "It's like I just got here from the moon," a Chinese graduate student newly arrived in the United States said. "Things are just so different here." He elaborated: he did not know what to expect of university teachers or administrators, of clerks in stores, of the bank teller, or of the government agents he supposed were everywhere.

Some people have little tolerance for ambiguity. They want to know what is happening; indeed, they may even want to be in control of what is happening. Such people are usually unhappy when they leave their own countries (if not their own home towns) because as foreigners they inevitably encounter ambiguous situations.

Tolerance for ambiguity is the ability to say to oneself, calmly, "Well, I don't know what's going on here. I'll just have to wait and see, or try to find out." People with a high tolerance for ambiguity have a much easier time in intercultural encounters than do those who feel a need to understand everything that is going on around them all the time.

TRAITS AND SITUATIONS

The waitress comes to your table, looks at you coldly, and says, "What do you want?!" You are startled by her unpleasant behavior. If you are like most people, you search your mind for an explanation for her conduct. One sort of explanation you might settle on has to do with the woman's personality traits: "What an unfriendly person!" you might say. Or, "She obviously doesn't like foreigners. She must be narrow-minded and prejudiced."

Another sort of explanation has to do with the woman's situation. Perhaps the other two waitresses who were supposed to be on duty failed to appear for work, and your waitress is trying to do three people's jobs. Perhaps her two teenage children had a loud argument about using the bathroom early that morning, and the woman was awakened from a deep sleep by the sound of their shouts. Perhaps another customer just yelled at her because the chef (not the waitress) had overcooked his meat. Any of these possible circumstances (and any of dozens of others) might account for the waitress' unfriendly approach to your table.

People's behavior stems from some combination of their *personality traits* and from the *situations* in which they find themselves. When we are familiar with other people, we know what their situations are—how their health is, what pressures they are under, what role they are currently in—and we are more likely to tolerate what might otherwise be unacceptable behavior from them. When we are unfamiliar with other people's situations, we tend to attribute their behavior solely to their personality traits. Often their traits explain far less about their behavior than their situations do.

In intercultural encounters, psychologist Richard Brislin

points out (see the bibliography), we typically know little if anything about other people's situations. We do not know them as individuals when we are new in their country. We do not know what their personal or work lives are like, and we do not know how they perceive what is going on around them. Since we are unfamiliar with their situations, we tend to attribute their behavior to their personality traits—this person is unfriendly, that one is prejudiced, the one over there seems nice, etc. By overlooking the influence of their situations on their behavior, we misunderstand and misinterpret much of what they do.

Having in mind the distinction between traits and situations helps foreign visitors remain aware that the reasons for other people's actions are complex and often unknowable. That awareness makes it easier to avoid misunderstandings and misinterpretations of what individual Americans do.

STAGES OF ADJUSTMENT

Another area in which scholars and researchers have done studies and failed to reach agreement has to do with the idea of stages of adjustment to a new culture. The general idea is that foreigners living temporarily in the States (or anywhere else) are likely to go through some fairly predictable stages. The first stage, according to most of these theories, is that of excitement and high energy. Next comes a period of letdown, of resentment, discouragement, depression, frustration, and perhaps hostility and rebellion. This stage, sometimes called "culture shock," is discussed below.

The third stage comes when the foreign visitor begins to learn and understand more about the host society and perhaps becomes better acquainted with some natives. In this stage the strength of the negative feelings diminishes and the person feels more competent and comfortable.

The final stage entails a general feeling of acceptance of one's place in the new situation, whatever that place may be.

Foreign visitors who are aware of the idea of stages of adjustment have a useful perspective on their own reactions.

They realize that their periods of intense happiness and excitement as well as their periods of animosity and depression are probably going to pass as they find their way to some reasonably stable accommodation with their new setting. They realize, too, that getting "adjusted" requires some time. (The word "adjusted" is in quotation marks because it is the word people usually use in this context, but its meaning is not at all precise. How do we determine, for example, whether someone is "adjusted" to a new setting? Can we say that person A is better adjusted than person B?)

D-I-E

"D-I-E" stands for Describe-Interpret-Evaluate. Referring to it as "D-I-E" makes it easier to remember. Remembering it can be very helpful. Many foreign students who have heard this idea have said it was the most helpful one they had encountered. Cross-cultural training specialists Milton and Janet Bennett say it is the single most important idea for visitors to other cultures to understand and employ.

"These Americans are crazy!" a visiting Brazilian engineer said. "They have no sense of humanity, of aliveness! They follow their rules like a bunch of robots. I've seen them out driving late at night when there are almost no other cars around. They come to a red light and they stop, even when there are no other cars within miles. They stop and they wait until the light turns green! They just aren't human!"

What has the Brazilian engineer told us about Americans? Almost nothing. Only that he saw at least one instance of an American stopping for a traffic signal when it was late at night and no traffic was in view. The rest of what the engineer said was his interpretation and evaluation of what he saw.

When they are talking about their experiences with others, people quite often blend description, interpretation, and evaluation in the way the Brazilian engineer did. For those in intercultural situations, learning to distinguish among those three types of reactions is most helpful.

Description has to do with what one actually *sees*, with

the "objective facts," with the events various observers agree took place. The engineer saw an American stop at a traffic light under certain conditions. Anyone who was with him at the time could have seen the same thing. If they were asked to describe the situation (without any interpretation or evaluation), they would all portray the same general scene. (This does not mean that eyewitnesses always agree. They do not. Different people notice different things. For example, a passenger with the Brazilian might have noticed what time it was when the car stopped, while the engineer himself was not aware of the hour.

Interpretation has to do with what one *thinks* about what one sees. The engineer thinks Americans are "crazy." He does not think it is necessary to follow rules when no one is around. Americans are too concerned about rules, he thinks. They are afraid to live spontaneously. That is his interpretation of what he saw, though, not what he saw. His interpretation is of course based on his own perceptions, assumptions, and values. Those perceptions, assumptions, and values are in turn based in part on his cultural background. Perhaps a Brazilian who stopped at that traffic signal under those conditions would be considered "crazy" by most Brazilians, but certainly not by most Americans. (Careful readers of this book will know why the American stopped at the signal.)

Evaluation has to do with what one *feels* about what one sees. The engineer feels that Americans are "un-human," not really alive. He feels uncomfortable around them, confined, unable to exhibit his personality. Once again, though, it is the engineer's values that are at issue, not the Americans' actual behavior. What the Americans would regard as good, law-abiding behavior the Brazilian feels is un-human. Which evaluation is correct? Neither, of course. It is strictly a matter of point of view.

Books about intercultural relations usually urge foreign visitors not to be judgmental. This is another way of stating what we are saying here about evaluation. Making judgments about other people's behavior is not usually constructive. Statements that contain the words "right," "wrong," "should," "ought," "better," and "abnormal" are usually evaluative or judgmental statements.

There are two things foreign visitors can do with the D-I-E idea. The first is to learn to distinguish, in their own reactions to other people, among Description, Interpretation, and Evaluation.

The second is to learn to stop, or at least delay, evaluating. Don't judge, or at least delay judging. We have seen that evaluations and interpretations are inevitably based on the visitor's own standards, standards that are based in part on his own culture. Those standards are frequently inappropriate in another culture. They lead to misunderstandings, misjudgments, and negative opinions. The Brazilian engineer got his descriptions, interpretations, and evaluations mixed together. The result was misunderstanding and unwarranted negativism. Had he been aware of the D-I-E idea, the engineer might have realized how he was misleading himself and reducing the likelihood that he would have constructive interactions with Americans.

CULTURE SHOCK

Culture shock can be described as the feeling of confusion and disorientation one experiences when confronted with a large number of new and unfamiliar people and situations. Many things contribute to it—smells, sounds, flavors, the very feeling of the air one is breathing. Of course, the natives' unfamiliar language and behavior contribute to it too. People's responses to culture shock vary greatly, from excitement and energetic action to withdrawal, depression, physical illness, and hostility. A particular individual might react to culture shock one way one day and another the next.

The notion of culture shock calls two useful points to mind. First, most people experience some degree of culture shock when they go to a new country, whether they admit it to themselves and others or not. Culture shock is more a product of the *situation* of being in a new culture than it is of the traveler's personal *traits*.

Second, culture shock, like other kinds of "shock," is normally transitory. It passes with time.

Academic analysts of the culture shock idea point out that the experience of culture shock need not be negative. While there may be some unhappiness and unpleasantness along with the confusion and disorientation, the confusion and disorientation are necessary steps in learning about the new culture. If everything in the new place is just like home, no learning will come from being there.

☆ ☆ ☆

CHAPTER 22

Activities for Learning
about American Culture

This chapter offers a large and diverse collection of activities that are intended to help foreign visitors learn more about American culture. A few of the activities are appropriate for short-term visitors, but most are intended for people who will be staying in the States for some time.

You are encouraged to do as many of these activities as you can—even ones that seem inconvenient or uncomfortable— because the potential benefits are great. Doing these activities can increase your understanding of Americans (and of yourself and people from other cultures as well), which means they can increase the likelihood that you will get maximum benefit from your stay in the States.

The first two items below are rather general and are extremely important. You should keep them in mind at all times. The subsequent items are more specific. They are not in any particular order of priority.

ASK QUESTIONS

Many foreigners are reluctant to ask questions of the natives. They feel embarrassed by their ignorance of simple things or by their limited English proficiency. It is important for you as a foreigner to remember that *you* are the one who suffers from your lack of knowledge of the local culture, society, and ways of doing things. The less you know, the harder everything is for you and the less likely you are to succeed in realizing the objectives of your visit. So when you have questions, ask them. If the first person you ask is not helpful (or patient, or whatever), ask another person. But ask.

Some of your questions will be requests for practical information. "Where is the closest service station?" for example, or "Where can I get my hair done?" But you can also ask more general questions. Ask people their opinions about things and about their experiences. Ask for their reactions to some of the generalizations about Americans that appear in this book. You will find that people have differing views about them, and you will begin to see that this book's stereotypes about Americans are indeed stereotypes, subject to exception and qualification.

LEARN AND PRACTICE LOCAL ENGLISH

Most Americans cannot use any language other than English. While they may admire a person who speaks more than one language, most of them do not place any value on learning another language themselves. They expect other people to learn or to already know *their* language, which of course is English. Foreign visitors who can speak and understand English will have a far better opportunity than non-English speakers to learn about the American people. "Local English" is the version of English spoken in the locality where a particular foreign visitor is staying. Although American linguists have a concept of "Standard American English," the fact is that there are regional and local variations with respect to idiomatic usage, colloquialisms, pronunciation (accent), rate of speech, and even aspects of communicative style (see Chapter Two). Foreign visitors other than tourists will want to learn the version of English that prevails in the part of the United States where they are staying.

There are many ways to improve your English:

Watch television (for Standard American English).

Listen to the radio.

Read a local newspaper.

Take an English class (helpful for beginners and low intermediate-level users of English, but less helpful at more advanced levels).

Hire a tutor.

Talk with anyone: neighbors, bus drivers, fellow bus passengers, people on the streets, fellow students, fellow workers, etc. Not all people will respond positively to your initiatives. Keep talking until you find people who do.

Make audiotapes of your own conversations. Listen to them and seek ways to improve the defects you hear.

Make audiotapes of things other people say in English (with their permission, of course), so you can review them.

Make a note of unfamiliar vocabulary and idioms you see or hear. Ask an American what they mean and learn them.

TAKE FIELD TRIPS

A field trip is a visit to a "real" place where you can observe what happens. Some of the field trips suggested below are for foreign visitors with particular interests (for example, businesspeople) or who are staying for a longer rather than a shorter time. Others are suitable for anyone.

Stand at a busy intersection. Watch the people and the cars. Listen. Here are but a few of the many questions you can yourself ask as you watch: How do drivers respond to traffic signals? How fast do the cars go? How do drivers proceed with left turns in front of on-coming traffic? How frequently do drivers honk their horns? For what reasons do they appear to use their horns? If traffic becomes obstructed, what do the drivers do?

Where do pedestrians walk? How fast do they walk? Do they touch each other? Where do they direct their eyes? How loudly do they talk? What do they do when they want to cross the street?

Observe parent-child interactions. In many of the field trip sites suggested here you will see children with their parents. Watch their interactions, and try to hear what they say. By what name do the children address the parents? What volume and tone of voice does each use? How do the parents convey their wishes or opinions to the children? The children to the parents? What do the parents do if the children behave in ways other than those the parents wish? How would all this compare to what you would see in a similar setting at home?

Observe male-female interactions. You can do this during the course of many of the field trips below. How old do the male-female pairs you see appear to be? Do older ones act differently from younger ones? How close do they get to each other? Do they touch? If so, how and where? Try to hear them talking, so you can tell what they are talking about and how they use their voices.

Go inside a public or commercial building, such as a bank, department store, or post office. How fast do people walk around? What do they do when more than one person wants attention or service from an employee? How close do they get to each other? How loudly do they talk? In what tones do employees and members of the public talk to each other? Where do they direct their eyes?

Go inside a restaurant. Take a seat and order a snack or beverage. Then watch and listen. How do the waiters or waitresses and the customers talk to each other—how formally? at what volume? How loudly do diners converse? What do they talk about? How do patrons get a waiter's or waitress' attention if they want additional service? What do patrons do to get their checks when they are ready to pay for their meals?

Sit in the reception area of a business or office. Watch and listen. How is the furniture arranged? What decorations are hung on the walls or placed elsewhere? How does the setting compare with a comparable setting at home? How do the employees interact with each other? Does their behavior change in the presence of customers? In the presence of high officials of the business? Try to hear what is said, and how it is said, when an employee answers the telephone. Do you notice any change in vocal volume or tone?

Attend an American business meeting. What is the furniture arrangement? Where do people sit, and what can you tell about participants' status vis-a-vis each other by the seating pattern? Who participates (speaks) in the meeting, and in what way? How long do people speak? Where do they look when they are talking and when they are not? Do they interrupt each other? Do some interrupt more frequently than others?

Board a public bus. Take a map, if you can get one, and try to follow the bus's route on it. But watch the passengers too. Notice where they sit, where they look, and how they talk (if they do).

Walk around a neighborhood, preferably the one in which you are living. What do you see in people's yards (if you are in a neighborhood where people have yards)? If people are in their yards, how are they dressed? What are they doing? What interactions among neighbors do you see? Do people leave their doors and windows open? Their curtains?

Visit a local school, especially if you will have children attending there. Talk with the principal, the counselor, and one or more teachers. Ask them all what role they want parents to play in their children's education.

Go to a drug store, a grocery store, and a department store. See what is available for sale there. Notice how merchandise is grouped (that is, arranged in categories) and how the prices are marked. Find an employee and get near enough so you can hear some interchanges between the employee and a customer. What tones do they use? What volume? How formal are they? How do customers behave at the place where they pay for goods they have selected? Find some customers who have small children with them. Get near enough so you can hear their talk. What do they call each other? How formal are they? How loud?

Attend a church service. What are others wearing? How do they act when they enter the building? Where do they sit? What do they do until the service begins? What does the religious official (minister, priest, rabbi, etc.) say and do? How does the congregation respond? What happens when the service ends?

Go to the local police station. Find an officer, explain that you are new in the community and are from another country, and ask what things the officer thinks it is important for you to know. Ask the *reasons* behind any pieces of advice whose rationale is not apparent to you. Notice how the officer treats you. Is the officer patient and courteous, in your opinion?

Attend a meeting of the city council (or whatever the local governing body is called). Sit next to someone who can answer your questions. Notice who else attends, what issues are discussed, and what arguments people offer to support their points of view. How do people treat each other? Who appears to be respected? Who is not taken so seriously?

Visit an American home, if you can get an invitation. (Many colleges and universities have "host family programs" through which foreign students are matched with local families who invite them for dinner and other family activities.) Notice the way the home is furnished—the types and arrangements of furniture and decorative items. How are you, as a guest, treated? Which rooms in the house do you have the opportunity to see? If you are being hosted by a couple, what can you tell about their division of labor? If children are present, observe the manner in which they and the adults treat each other. What topics do the hosts discuss with you? If the family has a dog, cat, or other pet that is not kept in an enclosure, you will be able to see how they treat the animal. If you are invited for dinner on Thanksgiving or Christmas, you will be able to see how a family celebrates those holidays.

Attend a sports event—a game of baseball, football, basketball, or whatever is convenient. Notice how the other people are dressed and how they behave. Are they attentive to the game, or to others in the audience? How do they display their reactions to what happens in the game? If you are watching a game you do not understand, ask someone sitting near you to explain it to you.

Go to a college or university classroom about 10 minutes before a class is scheduled to start, take a seat on the opposite side of the room from the doorway, and watch. What do the students bring with them as they arrive? In what part of the room do the early arrivals sit (if the teacher has not assigned each person a seat)? What do they do while waiting for the class to start? How do the students respond to the teacher's arrival? How does the teacher begin the class? If students arrive after the class has begun, what do they do? Besides taking notes on the lecture or discussion, what do students do during the class? As the class nears its scheduled ending time, what do the students do? What brings the class to a formal close and signals students to leave? (This field trip is especially beneficial for people who will be students in the United States.)

TALK WITH EXPERIENCED FOREIGNERS

There are advantages and disadvantages to becoming affiliated with the local expatriate community (if there is one). The advantages include the sense of identity and security you feel when you are around people who resemble you in important ways and who are sharing the experience of being a foreigner. One disadvantage is that time spent with other foreigners is time that cannot be spent with Americans. Another disadvantage is that you are likely to accept uncritically whatever misjudgments and misinformation have come to be perpetuated among the foreigners.

Try to find people who are from your country or world area, who seem to have a balanced and rational point of view, and who have been in the States for less than one year. (Those who have been here longer than a year are likely to have forgotten much of their initial experience, and so will not be able to be as helpful to you.) Ask them about their initial experiences: What things were most surprising? What was hardest to adjust to? Who had helped them the most? What field trips would they suggest? What other suggestions would they have?

Americans who have lived abroad, particularly ones who have lived in your own country, are likely to prove interested and helpful. You might be able to locate such people through a college or university international education office.

KEEP A JOURNAL

Keeping a journal is a time-honored way of coping with a new culture. Writing a journal forces you to be observant and to reflect on your experience, making it easier for you to distinguish among *descriptions*, *interpretations*, and *evaluations* of what you see. (Refer to the section in the previous chapter about D-I-E.) It gives rise to new questions you can ask others. In your journal you can relate your observations to the ideas you have found in this book, noting places where your experience is and is not in accord with what you have read here.

LEARN THE NAMES OF
LOCAL AND INSTITUTIONAL VIPS

Every community has its "very important people," the people who hold influential positions and whose names are likely to appear frequently in the newspapers and on radio and television news programs.

Learn the names of these VIPs:

Governor (of the state)

U.S. senators (each state has two)

U.S. congressman from the area where you are staying

Any other U.S. congressman or woman from the state who is well known

State senator from your area

State representative from your area

Mayor (or city manager) of your city or town

Local chief of police

Local sheriff

Prominent business leaders

Other prominent community leaders

Local celebrities (for example, media personalities and athletes)

Institutions such as businesses and universities have their own VIPs—the chief executive officers and other officers who hold influential positions.

You can learn the identities of these VIPs in various ways. Read the newspapers. Go to the library and either look up the information in publications or ask a librarian about it. The most direct way to get the information is to ask neighbors or other Americans you happen to meet. (Do not be surprised to

find Americans who cannot name their elected political representatives. You may well have to ask more than one person
before you get all the information you want.)

OBSERVE RITUAL SOCIAL INTERACTIONS

Notice what people say (and how they say it) and what they
do (and how they do it) when they:

greet an acquaintance,

take leave of an acquaintance,

are introduced to a new person, and

take leave of a person they have just met.

Watch for variations according to the age, sex, and apparent
social status of the people involved.

READ

Ask a librarian to help you find some publications about
local history and politics if you are at all interested in such
matters. (If the library is within a reasonable distance of the
place where you are living, apply for a library card while you are
there. How complex is the procedure? What documentation do
you need? How long does the procedure take? How does the
procedure compare to a comparable one at home?)

Read some of the publications in the bibliography at the
end of this book.

Read a local newspaper reasonably regularly. A feature of
local newspapers that can be particularly instructive for foreigners is the "advice column," in which readers' letters about
their personal problems are printed and then responded to. The
readers' letters convey a notion of the kinds of things Americans regard as problems. The advice columnist's replies suggest
and often explicitly state the values on which the reply is
based. (Notice how often the advice is to "mind your own business" or "confront the other person directly with your com-
plaint or point of view." This advice follows from the cultural
assumptions about individuality and openness that are dis-

cussed in this book. What other advice do you see that you can relate to ideas in this book?)

VIEW YOURSELF AS A TEACHER

Remember that most Americans are poorly informed about other countries and about the way their own country is viewed by foreigners. You can use your stay in the States as an opportunity to teach at least a few Americans something about your country and about a foreigner's reactions to America. Perceiving yourself as a teacher can help you remain patient (remember the importance of patience!) in the face of the many seemingly stupid questions Americans are likely to ask you, and which are often based on stereotypes, misinformation, or no information at all.

REFLECT

It may be stretching the point to include "reflecting" in a list of activities. But reflection is important in learning about a new culture, so it deserves explicit attention. To reflect, find a comfortable and quiet place, arrange to be uninterrupted for a while, and think about your recent experiences with Americans. Then ask yourself questions such as these:

What did I expect? How does my actual experience compare with what I expected?

What is happening to my stereotype of Americans? What commonalities do I see among them? What differences?

In thinking about and telling others about my experiences with Americans, am I carefully distinguishing among description, interpretation, and evaluation?

Am I judging too quickly? How often do I say or think the words "right" or "wrong" or "should" or "ought" when I consider what the Americans do?

Am I doing as much as I can to learn about the Americans and teach them about myself? What could I do to make my experience more interesting and constructive?

Conclusion

When I am working with a group of foreign students who are nearing graduation and getting ready to go home, I sometimes ask them to help me make a list, on the chalkboard, of those aspects of American life they would *not* like to take home with them. Some of the many items the students usually call out are these:

Excessive individualism

Weak family ties

Treatment of older people

Materialism

Competitiveness

Rapid pace of life

Divorce

"Free" male-female relations

Impersonality

Then I ask the students to list those aspects of American life they *would* like to see incorporated at home. A partial list:

Opportunity for individuals to raise their station in life

Efficiency of organizations

Hard work and productivity

Freedom to express opinions openly

General sense of freedom

Finally I ask the students to study the two lists and see if they notice any connections between them. After several moments someone will usually say, "Yes. Organizations are efficient because of the impersonality and the rapid pace."

Someone else will observe, "There would not be so much possibility for individuals to get better positions if family ties were stronger, if people had to stay where their parents are. People would not move around so much to get better jobs. Maybe even divorce is related to that!"

Another observation: "Maybe it's the materialism that leads people to work so hard." And another: "Individualism goes with the sense of freedom."

And so on. Most of the items on the don't-want list are related to items on the do-want list. So it is with the various aspects of what we call "culture." They fit together. They overlap. They reinforce each other. It is not possible to take one or two aspects of a culture and transplant them somewhere else. They will not fit.

Foreign visitors who make the effort to understand Americans will understand how various aspects of American culture fit together. They will see the patterns that underlie people's behavior. They will become able to predict what other people will do. Their interpretations will become more accurate. They will be less ready to judge. All this makes them better able to interact constructively with Americans and to achieve their purposes in visiting the United States.

Bibliography

People who want to pursue some of this book's topics in greater depth are referred to the publications listed below. The publications are in five categories: American culture, intercultural relations, readings for students, readings for business or professional people, and English-as-a-foreign-language texts.

AMERICAN CULTURE

Bellah, Richard, and others. *Habits of the Heart: Individualism and Commitment in American Life.* (Berkeley: University of California Press, 1985.) A historical and sociological analysis of contemporary American culture. Long, but well written and quite interesting.

Fussell, Paul. *Class.* (New York: Ballantine Books, 1983.) A witty and insightful discussion of social-class markers in America. Fussell relates social class to such matters as dress, speech, and home furnishings.

Liu Zongren. *Two Years in the Melting Pot.* (San Francisco: China Books & Periodicals, 1984.) A scholar from the People's Republic of China describes his two-year stay in the United States.

Lanier, Alison. *Living in the U.S.A.* (Yarmouth, ME: Intercultural Press, Inc., 1981.) A very practical guide to daily life in the United States, with some chapters especially for businessmen.

Slater, Philip. *The Pursuit of Loneliness.* (Boston: Beacon Press, 1970.) A critique of individualism in American life.

Stewart, Edward, and Milton Bennett. *American Cultural Patterns: A Cross-Cultural Perspective,* 2d ed. (Yarmouth, ME: Intercultural Press, Inc., 1988.) A revised edition of a widely-used analysis of American cultural assumptions and values as compared to assumptions and values that prevail elsewhere.

INTERCULTURAL RELATIONS

Brislin, Richard. *Cross-Cultural Encounters: Face-to-Face Interaction.* (New York: Pergamon Press, 1981.) Brings together and analyzes results of research on cross-cultural relations in many sectors. Very thoughtful comments and observations.

Condon, John and Fathi Yousef. *An Introduction to Intercultural Communication.* (Indianapolis: Bobbs Merrill, 1975.) Offers ideas about cultural differences and the psychology of intercultural interactions.

Lewis, Tom and Robert Jungman, Eds. *On Being Foreign.* (Yarmouth, ME: Intercultural Press, Inc., 1986.) A collection of short stories by various well-known fiction writers. Each story concerns an intercultural situation.

Morris, Desmond, and others. *Gestures.* (New York: Stein & Day, 1980.) Anthropological research on gestural communication, with cross-cultural comparisons.

Smith, Elise, and Louise Fiber Luce, Eds. *Toward Internationalism,* 2d ed. (Scranton, PA: Harper & Row Publishers, Inc., 1986.) Brings together 14 essays introducing various aspects of intercultural communication, including American values, culture shock, and nonverbal communication.

FOR STUDENTS

Althen, Gary. *Learning with Your Foreign Roommate.* (Iowa City: Office of International Education & Services, University of Iowa, 1981.) A primer on intercultural relations for foreign and American students who are roommates.

Barnes, Gregory. *The American University: A World Guide.* (Philadelphia: ISI Press, 1984.) The American system of higher education explained to people from other countries.

Van den Berghe, Pierre. *Academic Gamesmanship.* (New York: Abelard Schuman, 1970.) A sociologist's analysis of the workings of American universities.

FOR BUSINESS AND PROFESSIONAL PEOPLE

Adler, Nancy. *International Dimensions of Organizational Behavior.* (Belmont, CA: Wadsworth, 1986.) Addressed to Americans, but useful for anyone participating in business activity with people from other countries. Discusses the influence of cultures on attitudes and behavior in the business world.

Barnes, Gregory. *Communication Skills for the Foreign-Born Professional.* (Philadelphia: ISI Press, 1982.) Offers suggestions concerning nonverbal communication among Americans and explains some points about American English usage.

Moran, Robert and Philip Harris. *Managing Cultural Differences,* 2d ed. (Houston: Gulf Publishing Co., 1986.) A comprehensive guide for managers who supervise multicultural organizations or who do business with people from other countries.

ENGLISH-AS-A-FOREIGN-LANGUAGE TEXTS

An increasing number of EFL texts are based on the notion that learning English entails learning not just vocabulary and grammar but also learning about the culture of those who live in English-speaking countries. Such books include readings and exercises intended to instruct about cultural characteristics. Here are some examples:

Church, Nancy and Anne Moss. *How to Survive in the U.S.A.: English for Travelers and Newcomers.* (New York: Cambridge University Press, 1983.)

Coffey, Margaret P. *Fitting In: A Functional/Notational Text for Learners of English.* (Englewood Cliffs, NJ: Prentice-Hall, 1983.)

Levine, Deena R. and Mara Adelman. *Beyond Language: Intercultural Communication for English as a Second Language.* (Englewood Cliffs, NJ: Prentice-Hall, 1982.)

Zanger, Virginia. *Face-to-Face: The Cross-Cultural Workbook.* (Scranton, PA: Harper & Row Publishers, Inc., 1985.)

The best American source of publications on intercultural matters is Intercultural Press, Inc., P.O. Box 768, Yarmouth, ME 04096.